# Real Life

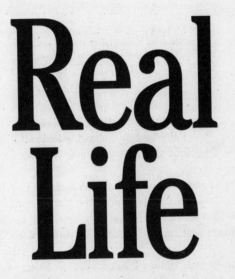

# Real Life

The Ten Things Every
Grown-Up Needs to Know

## TOM HEYMANN

FAWCETT COLUMBINE • NEW YORK

A Fawcett Columbine Book
Published by Ballantine Books
Copyright © 1994 by Thomas N. Heymann

All rights reserved under International and Pan-American Copyright Conventions. Published in the United States by Ballantine Books, a division of Random House, Inc., New York, and simultaneously in Canada by Random House of Canada Limited, Toronto.

Library of Congress Catalog Card Number: 94–94060

ISBN: 0-449-90688-4

Cover design by Kristine Mills
Text design by Ann Gold

Manufactured in the United States of America
First Edition: June 1994
10  9  8  7  6  5  4  3  2  1

*To my family and*
*the REAL love we share.*

# Contents

Author's Note ix

Acknowledgments xi

Introduction xii

1 Buying a Car 3

2 Buying a Home 25

3 Getting a Mortgage 53

4 Insurance and Planning Ahead 84

5 Caring for an Elderly Relative 135

6 Investing in the 1990s 176

7 Getting the Most for Your Money 215

8 Protecting Yourself and Your Money 236

9 Keeping Your Job 249

10 Credit: Staying Out of Trouble 263

Index 289

# Author's Note

*Real Life: The Ten Things Every Grown-Up Needs to Know* is an attempt to give readers the tools to deal with today's increasingly complicated world. This book grew out of my own frustration at constantly feeling overwhelmed by the many rapid-fire decisions required by modern life. Why, I asked myself, should I be making so many underinformed decisions about so many very important things. And why, I continued, isn't there any place, or any person, to go to for help.

The answer, I found, comes back to today's complicated world. In years past, things truly were simpler. Life was less complicated and people had more time to share with their friends and family. Time in which they could gain support from one another and learn from each other's personal experiences. Today, as we rush from place to place, we find ourselves with precious little time to consult with our friends and family about a widening array of important personal and professional matters. More than ever before, as we venture forward through adulthood, we're on our own.

*Real Life: The Ten Things Every Grown-Up Needs to*

*Know* is your family, your friends, and a few experts, all wrapped into one; sharing with you their wisdom, advice and personal experiences. *Real Life* combines actual research with anecdotal stories in a format that provides readers with the information that can help us all get through some of life's most difficult negotiations.

So when it seems like there's no place else to turn, you'll always have this book—your "Dr. Spock for grownups." So relax, enjoy, and learn how to gain some control over your life.

*Note:* All of the information contained in this book was verified and was believed to be accurate at the time the final manuscript was prepared. Pending federal, state, and local legislation, particularly in the areas of health care, investments, and taxation, may affect your particular situation. It is imperative that you obtain professional and/or legal advice before making important life decisions.

# Acknowledgments

I want to thank my friends and literary agents, Herbert and Nancy Katz, for their continued support and guidance; my editor, Elisa Wares, for her relentless enthusiasm; Alec Rabinowitz for his valuable assistance in getting this project started; and journalist Francis Flaherty for his contribution to the completion of this book.

The following individuals also provided invaluable input:

*Al Cardillo*   Executive Director,
    New York State Senate Committee on Health
*Robert W. Dumser*   Republic National Bank
*Paul A. Levis*   Registered Investment Advisor,
    Professional Financial Services, Yonkers, New York

# Introduction

*Real Life: The Ten Things Every Grown-Up Needs to Know* is a book about coming to terms with the reality around us—one that is markedly different from that which greeted our parents as they made their way into adulthood.

Many of us are facing a world of shrinking opportunities and radically revised dreams. A well-known 1980s beer commercial asked its yuppie audience, "Who Says You Can't Have It All?" The answer, already implicit in the question, was "Who would dare." The 1990s answer to this question might start with shrinking job opportunities, increased international competition, and a deflationary housing market, to name just a few.

It's a fact: As a whole, we're not going to live as well as our parents. Oh sure, some of us will. But a much larger number will need to call on parents and relatives for help with graduate school tuition, down payments on homes, nursery school tuition for our kids, etc. In a growing number of cases, we'll want our old rooms back. That symbolic light at the end of the tunnel is beginning to look to us more like a speeding train than a beacon of hope.

So what are we all to do? We can't give up. And we certainly can't turn back. While the deck of life may indeed be stacked against us, there are a number of things we can do to level "life's playing field." *Real Life: The Ten Things Every Grown-Up Needs to Know* is here to help.

We're all learning—the hard way—how difficult it is to grow up. There are jobs to be found, homes to be bought, children to be raised, responsible investments to be made, and an endless list of important decisions to be negotiated each and every day. With the help of this book, and some of your own common sense, you'll be able to carry some cards of your own and deal with today's cruel world on a more equal footing. The bottom line: You'll be able to achieve greater control over your own life. So let's get to it!

# Real Life

# 1 $ 🏠 🚗 🎓 ♥

# Buying A Car

## "Without Being Taken for a Ride"

**B**uying a new car can be one of life's most stressful undertakings. New cars are expensive, and the absence of set prices makes your preparation and negotiating skills a deciding factor in establishing what you pay. Remember, car dealerships do this every day. You, on the other hand, buy a new car every six or seven years.

As a new car buyer, you will be confronted with a dizzying array of models, prices, options, financing alternatives, etc. You must be prepared. With the average new car costing more than $16,000, poor preparation or uncertain negotiating can easily cost you thousands of your hard-earned dollars. Over the course of your car-buying career, this can add up to a handsome sum.

This chapter, complete with detailed instructions and a practical strategic game plan, will help you emerge from this REAL life battle with your ego intact, your dream car in hand, and your pockets a little less empty.

## Preparing for Battle

### 1. Get Acquainted with Price Information

Check newspaper ads, but read the fine print: These ads are designed to draw you in to a particular showroom, often enticing you with super low prices on demo models or special limited quantity promotional vehicles. Check consumer books and periodicals for the latest wholesale price estimates, both for the car itself and its available options. Good sources for this information include: Jack Gillis's *The Car Book*, and the Consumer Reports *New Car Buying Guide*.

### 2. Study the Car's Maintenance and Resale History

These guides will also provide estimates of the car's annual maintenance expenses and detail its historical resale value. Avoid new models, since they will not have a repair or resale history and, as a general rule, have more problems.

### 3. Scout Out Several Dealerships

Get recommendations on their business practices by speaking with friends and acquaintances, writing your state attorney general's office, and calling your local chapter of the Better Business Bureau. Find out if any complaints have been filed against the dealer and, if so, how they were resolved. If you plan to service your car at that dealership, you should also ask separately about its service department.

## 4. Test Drive a Rental or a Friend's Car

By borrowing or renting, you'll really get to know the car—its handling, comfort, and quirks. It sure beats a frenzied ten-minute test drive with a talkative salesperson strapped down in the seat next to you.

# Knowing Your Enemy

While their mothers may not agree, car salespeople are thought by many to be among the sleaziest individuals walking the face of the earth. They will do anything in their power—at least that's what we've been told—to extract the last pennies out of your pocket and, if necessary, put you into terminal debt. Here are some things you will need to know about your salesperson ("the enemy") before you enter the showroom ("the battlefield").

## 1. They Try to Manipulate Your Emotions

Car salespeople are regularly sent to training programs where they're taught how to get you, the buyer, to bite. Getting a commitment, according to the dogmatic training they receive, can be achieved with one very simple strategy: Let the buyer say it in his or her own words. They know that if a salesperson makes a statement about a car's better qualities, you will probably write it off as sales pressure. If YOU say it, however, it takes on a religious quality ... putting your pronouncements on a par with Moses speaking to the Israelites, or Jesus speaking to his disciples.

## 2. They Use Child Psychology to Sell Cars

Clever parents may say things like:

"Gabriel, do you want to put away your toys first or clean up the mess you made in the kitchen?"

Young children (at least before the age of Bart Simpson) don't usually know enough to answer:

"No, I'd like to go out for ice cream."

Adults, in the childlike state evoked by the power and prestige of the new car purchase, aren't likely to get nasty and condescending enough to tell the salesperson to shut up. Your next best defense then is to keep your feelings to yourself.

---

### REAL-LIFE DIALOGUE

SALESPERSON: "Are you looking for that BMW 320i in red or blue?"

BAD ANSWER: "Oh, I love red! It's my favorite color."

*BETTER ANSWER:* "It really doesn't matter."

---

## 3. They Try to Dazzle and Distract You

The auto showroom, with its flashy colors and dazzling lights, has a Las Vegas casinolike feel to it. So, as you would try to do on any "responsible casino visit," do not enter the showroom tired or intoxicated. While this may seem to you to be all-too-common sense, you'd be surprised at the number of fueled-up individuals who have traveled directly from their local tavern to their local car dealership only to leave holding a five-year loan on a "loaded" gas guzzler.

HOW DO THEY DISORIENT YOU?

- Shiny new cars that will never be that clean again.
- Huge American flags (they may be showing your country's flag, but always remember you're behind enemy lines).
- Circus tents and even circus animals—watch your step!
- Bogus sales that have no apparent beginning or end.
- Screaming ads that promise you the World—FOR NO MONEY DOWN!! (bikini-clad woman included, of course).

## 4. They Do Anything to Sell You a Car

Your salesperson may seem like a real nice guy or gal, you may even like them. BEWARE: Anything that comes out of your salesperson's mouth should be taken with a very large grain of salt.

### REAL-COMMON MISTRUTHS

MISTRUTH I: "There's only one of that model left in the state."

TRUTH: Even if that's true (unlikely), they'll be happy to get you one from a dealer in a neighboring state. Express your willingness to wait if it means getting a better price or a car with fewer unwanted options.

MISTRUTH II: "The manufacturer's prices are going up tomorrow. If you leave a deposit with me today, I'll lock you in at today's price."

TRUTH: They're willing to lie to make a deal. If you get nervous (that a price increase might indeed be coming), check with another dealer right away.

To win at this car-buying war, you'll need to know when to hold your ground, when to charge forward, and when to guard your flank against surprise attacks. One thing is for certain, you'll be rewarded for your preparation, patience, and perseverance (the three *P*'s of car buying). Try to remain flexible and observe the following rules:

- Don't fall in love with any one car.
- Don't make color an issue.
- Be willing to wait for the delivery of your car.
- Try to buy at the end of the month (dealers often need to meet monthly quotas and will be eager to deal).
- Try to buy last year's models (the delivery of new models will make a dealer anxious to move his inventory of "old" new cars).
- Be prepared to walk away from a deal.

The spoils of your victory will include the car and model of your choosing, a fair price, and acceptable terms and conditions. Not bad for a little extra work.

## Holding Your Ground

### 1. Let the Salesperson Do All the Talking
Try to avoid getting sucked into indicating exactly what it is you want in a new car. This is a situation similar to being arrested by Sergeant Joe Friday and Officer Gannon of "Dragnet":

*"Anything You Say Can and Will Be Used Against You"*

Your salesperson will focus on your utterances about monthly payments, financing needs, color, or the immediacy of your transportation needs. He or she will use your statements to steer you into buying a higher-priced model that coincidentally meets your blabbered priority. Remember, your personal preferences are nobody else's business but your own.

## REAL-LIFE DIALOGUE

SALESPERSON: "How much would you like to spend a month?"

BAD ANSWER: "I really need to keep my monthly payments under $300."

*BETTER ANSWER:* "I don't know."

If you tell your salesperson your maximum payment, you can be certain that the car you end up buying will have a monthly carrying cost within pennies of this amount. Keep your thoughts to yourself.

## 2. Look Out for the Model Shuffle

You have to balance your research with the emotional side of this process. If a salesperson, in the heat of battle, convinces you to change to a new model, all of your research becomes useless. If this happens it's time to call a time-out. Leave the game temporarily and go back to the drawing board. The car will still be there tomorrow. Often, salespeople will try to "steer you" into different models, particularly if they carry a higher price or come equipped with many standard options. Why? His or her sales commission on these cars will be higher. Moreover, your research, and your negotiating ability, will be impaired, turning you into a sitting duck.

## 3. Don't Close the Deal on the First Visit

Be warned: The dealer will try to get you involved in a negotiation right away. You're likely to hear the following real-life dialogue:

### REAL-LIFE DIALOGUE

SALESPERSON: "What will it take to get you to buy this car tonight?"

BAD ANSWER: "A really good deal."

*BETTER ANSWER:* "I'm not in a hurry."

## 4. Don't Rely on the Sticker Price

You probably already know that everyone pays a different price for a car. So you may bring in your copy of *Consumer Reports*, using it like a terror-struck victim in a low-budget horror film trying to repel Dracula with a cross. Car salespeople laugh at those of us who bring these guides into the showroom. Why? The guides, while serving as a useful starting point for your research, give the user a false sense of confidence. The wholesale prices given are merely averages, and automobile prices change frequently.

Remember: Dealer sticker prices can run between 10% to 20% over "dealer cost" (that illusive wholesale price). Generally speaking, the larger the car the greater the dealer markup. Margins on some luxury models, and certain pickups and vans, may be even higher. Dealers also receive factory "rebates" (kickbacks), equalling 3% or more of the sticker price on every car they sell. Special manufacturers' incentives make it even more difficult to unearth your dealer's real costs.

## REAL OXYMORONS

According to *Webster's*, oxymorons are figures of speech in which antithetical incongruous terms are combined. Some of my favorites:
- Jumbo Shrimp.
- Military Intelligence.
- Express Lines.
- "Great Sticker Prices."

## 5. Avoid Expensive Dealer Options

Dealer-applied undercoating is unnecessary and may actually harm the factory installed rustproofing that comes standard with most vehicles. Dealer sound systems are almost always overpriced. You'll get better quality, at more competitive prices, by shopping for this item separately. Also, if you refuse to accept the car's standard radio, you should be eligible for a refund—ask for it. Some "life-priority" items, like airbags and antilock brakes, may be a good idea. They may also entitle you to a discount

on your auto insurance and improve your car's resale
value.

---

## Taking Charge of the Battle

There are many things you can do to take control of the
car-buying negotiation:

### 1. Keep the Negotiations Separate

When you purchase a new car, you'll be tackling at least
two of the following negotiations:
- The actual price of the car itself.
- The car's options packages.
- The trade-in value of your old car.
- Financing.
- Extended warranties.
- Insurance.

Losing track of these issues is easy to do, but can be
deadly. A dealership can make all of its profit on a car by
simply arranging your loan or by out-foxing you on your
trade-in. Negotiate each deal separately and insist that
any discussion of trade-ins, financing, or warranties take
place AFTER you have reached a price on the car.

This way, you'll have more negotiating room in the
end. For example, if you decide to finance through the
dealer, you can do so on the basis of the relative merits,

and rates, of the lender it uses. If you decide to trade in your old car, you can do so in a separate negotiation.

## 2. Get Detailed Price Quotes from Other Dealerships

Shopping around will not only provide you with a greater understanding of the range of costs for the car, its options, financing, etc., but may also give you an extra offensive edge. How? The thought of losing a sale to a rival dealership can really get to them. Don't be shy about making your efforts to shop around known to the dealer.

Of course, shopping at different dealerships for the exact same car is smart, but you'll have to be pretty tough not to get hooked by the first dealer who offers you a deep discount. Let the deal stand, despite his claims that it is contingent upon an immediate close, until you have a chance to reevaluate the specifics and do more comparison-shopping. You can try but, unfortunately, dealerships will not usually let you shop for a car over the phone. They know very well that getting you into their showroom is half the battle.

## 3. Try an Outrageously Low First Offer

Dealers typically trade cars with one another, and manufacturers are always making deals in order to control overstocked inventories. So don't be shy about a low offer; you'll never know until you try. They're certainly not going to throw you out of their showroom.

## 4. Don't Give a Deposit

The $100 deposit routine is a "commitment-seeking" ploy.
It simply doesn't make a bit of difference to your deal
(except to your salesperson who is well aware that the
very act of handing over a "refundable" deposit makes
you many times more likely to end up driving home in
one of his or her cars).

## Guarding Your Flank

There are many other issues and negotiations surrounding your new car purchase that will have a REAL bearing
on your future happiness as the owner of a new car. We
call this section "Guarding Your Flank."

## 1. Itemize . . . Itemize . . . Itemize: Every Possible Option

Before you accept the car, or start talking over financing,
examine each component of the bill. You'll have to watch
the options and add-ons like a Pit Boss in a Vegas casino.
You should be up-to-date on the wholesale prices of each
option. Door guards, for example, are basically no-cost
items. This kind of add-on contributes to an average per
car profit to the dealer of well over $1,000.

## 2. Get a Fair Price for Your Old Car

If you have the time, selling your old car yourself will
usually get you a better price. WARNING: Using guidebooks which estimate used car values can be tricky. Your

car is unique. Get several assessments of its value from guidebooks (the Consumer Reports *Guide to Used Cars*, or *Edmund's Used Car Prices*), classified ads, or a mechanic's appraisal (probably about $50). BEWARE: Dealerships get cheap thrills from convincing people that their cars are worthless (they may even have the gall to tell you that it will cost them money to have it taken away). They then proceed to make a handsome profit by cleaning up and reselling your "worthless" car.

## REAL TIP

Don't take cash in exchange for your old car. Better idea: Have the purchase price reduced by the amount of your trade-in. This will reduce your total purchase price and save you money in taxes.

## 3. Consider Several Financing Sources

Four out of five new-car buyers use dealer financing. Why? Because it's more convenient. Know however that dealers love to provide you with financing. It's easy money to them. All they have to do is make a phone call and have you fill out some paperwork.

## REAL-LIFE DIALOGUE

SALESPERSON: "What are your financing needs?"
BAD ANSWER: "I haven't made any arrangements yet."
*BETTER ANSWER:* "I'm self-financing."

By staying quiet, you'll retain more control when it comes time to discuss financing, which is *after* the purchase price of the car has been decided. You should compare their rates with those being offered by your credit union and local financial institutions. You may also want to consider a second mortgage on your home as a way to finance your new-car purchase. Advantage: The interest on home loans is deductible. Disadvantage: You're borrowing money against your home to purchase a depreciating asset.

Car financing discounts ("1.9% on select cars," etc.) are usually roughly equal, depending on the amount being financed, to any cash discount or "rebate" being offered. Negotiate your purchase price without any discussion of these promotional incentives, then ask for your discounted loan or rebate. BEWARE: Your salesperson will try very hard to integrate these marketing gimmicks into the negotiation right from the start.

## 4. Get a Short-Term Car Note

By definition, a car loan is a short-term consumer loan. The longer the term the lower your monthly payments but the greater the interest you will pay over the life of the loan. More than half of today's new-car loans are five years in length. And whereas the average new-car loan in 1970 averaged just 34.7 months, that average grew to 54 months today. Why? Because more buyers can only handle the lower monthly payments that come with a longer loan. The problem is, however, that the maintenance costs on your car will rise as the car gets older. Also, your car may reach a state of "negative equity" (be worth less than your outstanding loan amount) when you want to trade it in for a new model. As a general rule, try to keep your loan term to four years or less. Either put more money down or buy a less expensive car. You'll be happier in the long run.

## 5. Leave the Leasing to Donald Trump

For many of the reasons given above, leasing is growing in popularity. Seduced by little or no-money-down deals, and relatively low monthly payments, Americans are leasing cars in record numbers. Today, nearly one in three new cars is leased. Why? Because more Americans are facing difficult financial times. Leasing allows a driver to get a new car without having to come up with a large down payment. It also allows him or her to drive "more car for the money." Either way, remember that leasing simply defers the pain of buying a new car.

If you buy the car instead, you'll have the chance to either drive payment-free for several years after the loan is paid off; or benefit from the cash value provided by a trade-in or personal sale.

Manufacturers have been placing more emphasis on leasing. And some promotional leasing deals may actually make financial sense on paper. But before you jump into your new Ferrari (just $499 a month!), make certain that you negotiate your lease deal as carefully as you would a new car purchase. And be sure to consider the following points:

WEAR AND TEAR

You'll be responsible for any damage to the car and you may get into a hassle over what is "reasonable wear and tear." As the owner of two large dogs, and the father of two small children, the prospect of facing financial scrutiny and accountability for "scuffed" or "worn" seats is truly terrifying.

MILEAGE CHARGES

The worst aspect of leasing may be the fact that you're charged for excess miles over, on the average, 10,000 to 15,000 miles a year. Penalty charges can be as high as 8 cents to 10 cents per mile! You'll be constantly thinking about this restriction as you drive—eyes glued to the odometer.

The worst case scenario is that you'll have some unforeseen change in your lifestyle, such as a job transfer, which requires more driving. By the way, in case you were wondering, you don't get a refund if you drive fewer than the allotted number of miles—surprise!

REPAIRS

You'll also be responsible for any major repairs which aren't covered by the car's warranty ... and then you have to give them back "their" car.

EARLY TERMINATION PENALTIES

Lease deals also carry very expensive penalties for early termination. Make certain that your agreement includes reasonable estimates of your liability as the lease term progresses.

So, by leasing you're really embarking on a Trumplike, go-for-broke, 1980s, buy now–pay later, mentality. And after your four years of leasing, when your friends have paid off their new car loans and are driving payment-free, you'll probably feel worse than "The Donald" when they took away his casinos and his mega-yacht.

## 6. Avoid Extended Service Warranties

Extended service warranties extend your car's original warranty farther into the future and/or cover certain repairs that may not be included in your manufacturer's warranty. They're offered by manufacturers, and a few independent companies. Coverage can range in price from $250 to $750. The warranties can also vary in terms of coverage and duration.

As a result of increased competition in the automotive industry, manufacturers' new-car warranties have improved significantly. Consequently, it is likely that much of the coverage provided by any extended warranty will duplicate much or all of your free coverage.

If you do decide that you need the additional "*feeling* of safety" provided by an extended warranty, make certain you purchase a policy from a reputable dealer or a well-financed national company. Be certain to review the following points before you sign an agreement:

- What, exactly, does the warranty cover, and for how long?

- Is there a deductible (one time OR per event)?
- Does the company reimburse YOU for repair expenses or pay the repair shop directly (the latter is obviously better)?
- Does the policy provide you with a replacement car when yours is in the repair shop?
- Does the policy pay for towing?
- Can you use any repair shop you choose?

## 7. Shop Around for Insurance

Your dealership may also try to sell you insurance. As with financing, you will almost always get better rates by shopping around. In any event, keep any discussion of insurance separate from your other negotiations.

# Final Victory

At this point you are hopefully celebrating the purchase of your new car. As we all know, however, problems can arise in any negotiation. If you have any problems with the dealer that can't be easily resolved, make certain that you protect your rights. If you get into a dispute, and you have a specific problem which you can document, threaten to write to your office of consumer protection (usually run by your state attorney general's office, but in some states administered by county governments). If you don't get any immediate satisfaction from your salesperson, talk to his or her boss: the sales manager. If the sales manager doesn't help, go to his or her boss: the owner. If the owner is unresponsive, contact the manufacturer's regional office. Send a copy of all correspondence to the president of the company and be sure to include complete documentation of your problem. Include dates, names, events, and copies of any key documents.

As a next step, work through your government agencies or the Better Business Bureau. Finally, if all else fails, contact a lawyer. Lemon laws are administered on a state-by-state basis so you'll have to ask your lawyer, or your attorney general's office, about your state's current provisions. One final note: If you are asked to resolve your dispute in an arbitration proceeding, make certain that you do not give up your right to sue in court at a later date.

## A Few Words About Used Cars

The high price of new cars has stimulated a surge in the sale of used ones. The National Automobile Dealers Associations (NADA) tells us that, for the first time since World War II, used cars now outsell new ones at franchised dealerships. With the average new car selling for about $16,000, it may make sense to consider a "preowned" car.

*Real Question: "Would You Buy a Used Car From This Man?"*

In addition to new-car dealerships, other sources for used cars are:
- Private sellers.
- Used-car dealerships.
- Rental-car agencies.
- Leasing companies.
- Auctions (Warning: Avoid these unless you're a qualified mechanic—you're generally not given a chance to take the car for a test drive or get an appraisal).

Many of the *advantages* of buying a used car are readily apparent:
1. *A lower initial cost.* The average used car sells for $8,000, leaving more of your money free for other uses—like paying off your credit cards.
2. *Lower insurance costs.* Your car will have a lower value and be less expensive to insure.

The *disadvantages* of buying a used car also need to be considered:
1. *Unknown repair histories.* Even if the seller presents you with repair records, you'll never know if any major problems were conveniently omitted. It may also be difficult to tell if the car was ever involved in an accident.
2. *Unknown driving histories.* Even if the seller looks and acts like Mother Teresa, you'll never know if she drove to church like Mario Andretti. This point is particularly important with the purchase of a used car from a rental agency.

3. *Higher initial maintenance costs.* Used cars are more likely to need expensive repairs.
4. *Lower reliability.* In general, used cars will break down more often.

To protect yourself from the many unknowns surrounding the purchase of a used car, be certain to follow these steps before writing a check for that "Cream Puff":

1. *Check the model's price history.* Books like the Consumer Guide's *Complete Guide to Used Cars*, the Consumer Reports *Guide to Used Cars*, Jack Gillis's *Used Car Book*, and *Edmund's Used Car Prices* will give you estimates for each model. Remember though, these are only estimates. Every car will be different.
2. *Check the model's repair and recall history.* The books listed above will give you some insight into the car's general repair, safety, and recall history.
3. *Check out the dealer.* If you're buying from a private company, check them out using your local Better Business Bureau or state and local consumer agencies.
4. *Test drive the car in all driving conditions.* Taking the car around the block will tell you little about the car's overall performance. Drive the car on the highway and in stop-and-go traffic. Listen for any strange noises and feel for any pulling or hesitation.
5. *Check the car's service records.* They will tell you how well the car has been maintained and alert you to

the existence of any other owners. Be wary if no records are available.

6. *Get a mechanic's appraisal.* Have your mechanic assess the car's value and detail any needed repairs. A mechanic may also be able to tell you if the car was ever involved in a major accident.

7. *Examine the car's warranties.* If you buy a used car from a dealer, it may come with a warranty protection plan. Many states now actually prohibit a dealer from selling a used car "as is." Examine what the plan does and does not cover, and for how long. Also remember that a used car may still be covered under the manufacturer's original warranty. Check to see if the warranty is transferable to a new owner and find out exactly what it covers.

# Buying A Home

## "Can I Afford It?
## Does it Still Make Sense to Own?"

Getting Real about real estate in the 1990s demands that you take a fresh look at all of your assumptions about this subject. Our generation has bought into the myth that real estate values will always rise. And why not: Throughout most of our lives, real estate has done nothing but go up in value.

The entry of baby boomers into the housing market caused prices to rise in a hurry, particularly in the 1970s when homes averaged a rousing 18.6% gain in value each year. A spin-off myth developed quickly: Buy a small crummy house or condo, anything that has a deed, hold it for a couple of years, and use your profits to get into a larger home. Then do it again, and again. But times have changed and it's important to take a fresh look at our assumptions about buying real estate.

## Understanding Market Values

In the 1970s, many fortunate people made killings in real estate. The housing industry thrived, particularly in rapidly growing urban and suburban centers. In the 1980s, prices began to stabilize nationwide, but not until certain urban areas, like Los Angeles, New York, Washington, and Boston, had experienced episodes of real estate fever. Prices actually tripled in some "hot" neighborhoods.

Since most real estate investments are made with other people's money (mortgage money), speculative booms can quickly get out of hand. Individuals who get on the bandwagon too late in the boom, paying over-inflated prices, often get stuck.

## 1. Why Real Estate Booms Get Too Hot to Handle?

Take a look at the numbers. You buy a house for $100,000 in the middle of a boom. The house goes up a cool 20% in one year and you find yourself owning a house that's worth $120,000. If you put down 10%, you now have a $20,000 gain from just a $10,000 investment. That's an amazing return for just one year: 200%.

But just as quickly as real estate speculation can get out of hand, markets can fall apart and experience rapid price declines. Why? Returns like 200% beat all other investments, drawing all buyers into the market. In order to get in on more of the action, buyers purchase the biggest and most expensive homes they can, taking on the largest mortgage payments they can qualify for.

The booming real estate market is like a hungry shark: Quickly, all spare money is eaten up. To make matters worse, any available land is quickly targeted for construction. Builders aren't stupid. They rush to cash in on higher prices too. The result: The supply of new homes rises just as the pool of qualified buyers is becoming exhausted (there are fewer new families around to enter the housing market). These combined forces inevitably burst the bubble.

## 2. The Horror: When Home Prices Decline

Say that house you just bought for $100,000 drops 20% in value instead. Now you can only sell it for $80,000 (minus selling expenses). The average fee for selling is about 6%, or $4,800. You'll have to spend some bucks to get the house prettied up for sale, too. Let's say you spend a modest $200 to do some painting and plant some pretty flowers.

Under this very possible REAL-LIFE scenario, where you've put down 10% and property values have declined by 20%, you've lost a depressing 250% on your investment.

THE CALCULATION

$20,000 (fall in price from $100,000 to $80,000)

+

$5,000 (your cost of selling and fixing up the home)

= $25,000 (your loss)

Now compare this amount to your down payment:

$25,000 loss compared with $10,000 investment =
$25,000/$10,000 = −250%

## 3. Conclusion: Real Estate Can Be a High Risk Investment

You must always be prepared for the possibility that you won't be able to sell your home at precisely the time you want, or for the amount you desire.

---

# Renting Versus Buying

There are many hard-and-fast rules regarding your decision to buy or rent. Like all hard-and-fast rules, however, there are many exceptions, and important variables to consider:

## 1. When Does it Make Sense to Rent?

The following advice is sort of un-American, if you accept the myth that it's an American responsibility to be a proud homeowner. Renting does mean putting up with a landlord and having someone over you, as the name implies. However, based on current trends, it may be the smarter financial choice for many. So when should we opt for a lease?:

### A. IF HOME PRICES ARE STAGNANT OR DECREASING

Unless home prices are on the rise, you'll end up having to pay for most or all of the mortgage closing costs and the commissions on the property's sale out of your own pocket and not out of your profits on the home. If home prices are falling, renting is considered by many experts to be a smart move.

### B. IF YOU ARE LIKELY TO MOVE WITHIN SEVEN YEARS

You are, on the average, likely to lose money on home ownership if you move within seven years. Consider the mortgage closing costs and your real estate selling expenses (typically 6%). If you think you might get transferred in a few years, wait to buy until both you and the real estate market are very "stable."

### C. IF YOU'RE IN THE 15% TAX BRACKET

Much of the financial advantage of owning real estate comes from the tax-deductible interest you pay on the mortgage. If you're in a relatively low tax bracket, you make much less use of this benefit.

## 2. When is Real Estate a Great Investment?

### A. WHEN HOME PRICES ARE RISING
### FASTER THAN THE RATE OF INFLATION

Remember, you'll need at least enough profit from your home to cover all your closing, selling, and moving expenses. If home prices in your area are on the rise, and you plan to stay for at least seven years, buying makes sense.

### B. WHEN YOU'RE IN THE 28% TAX BRACKET AND
### PLAN TO STAY IN THE HOME FOR AT LEAST SEVEN YEARS

It's hard to lose under this scenario: You're getting a great tax break on the mortgage interest and you have a relatively long horizon to weather any short-term price declines.

C. WHEN IT MAKES SENSE FROM A PERSONAL PERSPECTIVE
This issue can never be overstated. Renting is by definition a transient state. If you have a family, it's impossible to calculate the value, in cash terms, of the sense of stability that comes with home ownership: schools, friends, neighbors, etc.

# How Much Should You Spend?

Always maintain a cushion. Make sure that home ownership expenses don't cost you the lion's share of your budget. You should still be able to save and invest in other ways besides real estate. It's often said that your annual income should be about equal to half of your total mortgage amount. Another formula: Your mortgage, property taxes, utilities, and maintenance shouldn't exceed 36% of your gross income.

Don't think of real estate as the only way you're likely to accumulate long-term savings. On a 30-year mortgage, you'll be paying mainly interest during the first ten years. You may be able to win if home prices in your area rise, but you shouldn't rely on inflation to save the day— not in today's economic climate. If paying for a home sucks you dry financially, you're simply "putting all of your eggs in one basket."

---

# Selecting an Agent

---

Try to find a real estate agent who has an appreciation for your personal tastes—it will save you a great deal of time while shopping. The agent you want is a good listener, aggressive about seeking new listings and able to understand your sense of aesthetics. Try a test run with at least one agent recommended by a friend, relative, or professional contact. Describe in detail your likes and dislikes. See if you still end up spending a Sunday seeing contemporary homes which, as you had politely informed the agent, "turn your stomach."

If your message doesn't get through, the agent is either out to lunch or trying to double his or her commission by steering you toward his or her agency's "listings." Listings are homes which entered the market through their firm—meaning a full commission (from both buyer and seller) to that agency. These listings generally have their agency's "for sale" signs in front. It's routine to show you these first, even at the risk of turning you off. If you're not completely happy with your agent, find another.

## 1. Beware: Real Estate Agents Represent Sellers

Always remember that agents—both the seller's and the buyer's—have an obligation to work on behalf of the seller, i.e., get the highest price. More states are now requiring that agents make you fully aware of this fact, but it's important to keep this in mind as you shop. Agents make their living by being friendly to you, they want you to think of them as part of your family. The reality, however, is quite another matter.

You've got to play it close to the vest with these angels of mercy. Don't detail how much you've got to spend. This may be tough: They'll undoubtedly quiz you about your income, job history and down payment parameters—the basics of qualifying for a mortgage. You can't really blame them for trying to see if you're only window-shopping. Millions of Americans consider shopping for real estate a favorite hobby—right up there with mall-walking.

## 2. Discount Your Real Estate Agent's Optimism

Real estate agents in the 1970s and 1980s were fond of making statements like:

> "Don't worry about how much the house
> costs, real estate prices never go down.
> You'll always be able to sell it at a profit."

During the 1970s and most of the 1980s, making these statements was considered "acceptable behavior." As long as anyone could remember, real estate prices hardly ever declined.

## 3. The Agent Must Present to the Seller Any Offer You Make, No Matter How Ridiculous

Don't fall for the agent's line: "I wouldn't insult the owner with an offer that low." In a flat market, anything within

20% of the market, or going-price range, should be taken seriously. If your lowball offer is for real, then the agent has a legal duty to the seller to relay it.

## THE "GETTING REAL" GUIDE TO REAL ESTATE BUZZWORDS

"COZY" = Tiny

"MUST BE SEEN TO BE APPRECIATED" = Too expensive to put in print

"CONVENIENT LOCATION" = Next to a superhighway

"HANDYMAN'S SPECIAL" = Present owner doesn't have a clue as to how to fix it

"POPULAR NEIGHBORHOOD" = Pricy and, if you're status-oriented, you might fall for it

"NEEDS TENDER LOVING CARE" = Bring a bulldozer, the property should probably be leveled

"RUSTIC" = Looks like a backwoods shack

## Going It Alone

Dealing directly with the owner can be ideal because you can actually get the property cheaper. If you and the seller are not using realtors, somebody is saving about 6% of the sale price. In an ideal situation, you and the seller should both gain about 3% of the market values for similar houses in the neighborhood.

Buying a home without an agent or buying an FSBO (for sale by owner) can have its problems though: You may be faced with attempts by the seller to cover up defects, sudden changes of mind, and unpredictable delays of all sorts. The realtor's professional role as a facilitator of quick and efficient closings is likely to make the purchase process smoother. Real estate agents also have, in most states, a legal duty to reveal defects of which he or she is aware.

If you do decide to go this route, be sure to have an attorney, an appraiser, and a building inspector on your team. Good news: Certain states are working to broaden the rules regulating an owner's conduct when selling without a realtor.

## Getting Started: Casing the Market and Assessing Prices

Selecting a home is an emotional experience. However, many experts like to think of the home-buying process as being similar to waiting for a bus—there'll be another one along any minute. They argue that, in order to negotiate successfully, you must be willing to lose a home you've fallen in love with. Some like to characterize the process as learning to avoid the teenage crush syndrome.

Commonly, home buyers, even the most rational of souls, seem to reach a point where their emotions take over and all advice from well-meaning advisors is ignored. Why? The answer lies in the fact that each house is unique. A sentimental attachment grows. Perhaps it's the woods in the back, the hammock on the porch, or maybe just the color of the wallpaper. You become convinced that no other home has the magic of this one you've embraced. If this happens, for God's sake— and your bank account's—lie down, put your head between your knees, and breathe deeply. Do anything you can until these powerful feelings pass.

## 1. Evaluating a Property

If you're not familiar with a town, spend some quiet time in the library looking at the business and real estate sections of the Sunday newspaper. The worst thing you can do is rush into a market which is experiencing a decline in real estate prices.

Scout out the town's schools, municipal services (trash, sewer, police, and fire) and general environment; anything having to do with the air, land, or water quality that may affect your well-being in a new home. The smell of baking bread may seem nice as you drive by on the interstate, but it could drive you nuts if you had to smell it twenty-four-hours-a-day. Anything that generates noise, dirt, or odors—or attracts large numbers of people— should be suspect.

### A. THE QUALITY OF THE SCHOOLS

The reputation of a school system can make or break housing prices in a community. Widely followed indicators of the quality of a school system include the percentage of kids entering college upon graduation, average math and reading scores, and the student-faculty ratio. Ask your agent for a report on the school systems in all the areas you have under consideration.

Also, find out if the school system is short of funds. Is the school board in a constant battle with the town for more money or does it enjoy the community's full support when it comes to funding new programs? You may end up paying higher taxes for a strong school system, but your home's higher resale value will more than compensate for this expense.

---

## REAL QUESTION

"Should I care about the schools even if I don't have any children, or plan to have any?"

ANSWER: Yes, absolutely! If your town's schools are on the decline, you lose, too. The direction of local real estate values can be strongly influenced by its schools.

---

B. THE 11TH COMMANDMENT OF REAL ESTATE BUYING:
ASK THY PROSPECTIVE NEIGHBORS

Who else is going to reveal all the strange things that go on in a neighborhood? Listen to everything they say and try to note what problems are dismissed as being no big deal. Remember, there's a real tendency for homeowners, especially those who are trying to sell their home, to deny the truth regarding any negative aspects of his or her home or neighborhood.

## 2. Playing Detective:
## Track Actual Selling Prices

Get acquainted with prices of homes having roughly the same square footage and lot size. Classified ads will only tell you the asking prices, usually 10% or 20% higher than the probable selling price. You'll have to go elsewhere to get the skinny on actual selling prices. It's public information, so don't be shy about getting any prices you want.

Ask your agent for a "competitive market analysis" listing current asking prices, and recent sales prices, for similar homes. In some communities, selling prices are listed in the newspapers serving that area. They can also be found at the town hall and in the county's hall of records. Bear in mind that there is usually a passage of time before prices make their way to print. So, if you're hoping to track very recent sales, a trip to the town's records bureau may be necessary. You also should be aware that seasonal fluctuations can be critical to housing markets; the spring is historically the busiest season, particularly in colder climates. You're likely to get a better price during slower seasons. Get a Multiple Listing Service print-out from your agent to get a sense of local seasonal sales trends.

## 3. Getting an Appraisal

Real estate appraisers aren't licensed by any government agency. Find a company that's certified by one of the leading national appraising associations such as The American Institute of Real Estate Appraisers or the Society of Real Estate Appraisers. Cost of an appraisal: $175 to $300. NOTE: If your appraiser is on your mortgage lender's approved list, you may not have to pay for a second appraisal when your mortgage is processed.

## 4. Getting a Seller to See the Light About Prices

As a buyer of real estate, you're going to meet sellers who insist they won't sell unless they achieve a certain profit level or at least break even—they're not going to take a loss on their property. You may even feel sorry for these distressed sellers, maybe even going so far as to overpay by vast amounts of money. The thing you have to remember is that a seller's misconceptions should have nothing to do with determining a home's market value. Economics, particularly the forces of supply and demand, should determine real estate values. An appraisal can help to make the seller more realistic in pricing his or her home.

Here's a typical conversation about an unrealistic asking price:

THE REALTOR: "The reason your house has not sold over the last year and a half is because your asking price is simply out of touch, unrealistic, pie-in-the-sky, for today's more value-driven buyers."

THE SELLER: "When I bought this house four years ago, you said it was a steal. All I want is the chance to break even. I won't sell it for a penny less than the price I paid plus enough to cover the 6% fee your real estate company gets for acting as my sales agent."

YOU (THE BUYER): "I'm sorry but I can only pay what the market dictates the home is worth. I'm basing my offer on the results of an independent appraisal."

## 5. A Final Word on Finding the Perfect Home

Homes, like cars, are often used to define an owner's personality. You are what you buy. The important thing to remember is to keep your whims—say to buy a farm in the country or move to the mountains and commute two hours to work—under control. If you're contemplating a change—a new housing lifestyle, a longer commute—or you simply can't find the exact property you like, rent a house in the area while you check out farm life, sample the longer commute, or continue to search for your dreamhouse.

## Caution in Signing Contracts

Every real estate contract involves serious, long-term financial commitments. There is simply no way around it: You must find a lawyer who is adept at local real estate law to look over your shoulder, making sure that you are protected. Always use the lawyer as a shield if a seller or agent is pushing you.

The contract for the sale of real estate is the blueprint for the documents to follow. One of the reasons you need a lawyer is to make sure that you are proceeding carefully through these steps, and not binding yourself legally until it's absolutely necessary.

# The Condition of the Home

## 1. The Seller's Duty to Disclose Major Defects

Under these legal requirements—in force in a growing number of states—the owner of a property is required to inform the buyer about any problems. Obviously, a seller may not be eager to let you in on the home's problems, particularly if they're having trouble selling.

In most states, the real estate agent must also let you know about any property defects of which he or she is aware. This is often called "the leaky basement rule." A seller might just conveniently forget to tell the agent about some things, like the fact that the plumbing always backs up or the roof is a fire trap. The courts are working to resolve the issue of what agents should know and disclose. It's tricky to prove that an agent was aware of a problem. If the seller fails to disclose a defect or problem, knowingly or not, you may be able to seek compensation under your state's guidelines. Ask your lawyer about the regulations in your state.

## 2. Getting an Independent Inspection

Start by asking your lawyer or real estate agent for a referral. The American Society of Home Inspectors (ASHI) is noted for its code of ethics. Try to use one of its members.

A full home inspection will cost you about $300 (more if it's a large home), and it's a wise investment. An inspection may be your only prepurchase source of information about hidden defects and the potential need for extensive remodeling or repairs. Remember: New homes require inspections as well.

Try to join your inspector as he or she goes through the house, checking the roof, plumbing, wiring, and structural elements. Ask lots of questions—it's relatively inexpensive advice from an expert—and bring along a notepad and a pen. I learned an enormous amount from our inspector during our ninety minutes together.

## 3. Warranties and Buyer Protection Programs

As an added incentive to get you to buy a particular property, some homeowners and real estate agencies offer warranties or buyer protection programs on appliances and other mechanical components of a house. According to the National Home Warranty Association, more than half a million home warranties, costing between $250 and $400 each, were sold in 1990. The question to ask yourself is how much of this coverage are you likely to use, and how much are you willing to pay for this added insurance.

Depending on their age, many of the appliances covered by these programs may still be under the manufacturers' original warranties. Also, try to determine if the company offering the warranty is stable. Have they been in business long enough to be checked out? Try to get some references and see if you can speak to a few homeowners who have used the program and had to get reimbursed on a repair. Be sure to check the company's record by contacting your state or local department of consumer affairs and the Better Business Bureau office in your region. Also, consider whether the plan's deductible makes it unlikely you'll ever use the warranty.

If the warranty is included "free" with the house, it's going to be very difficult to determine how much you're paying for this extra. See if you can buy the house without the warranty, for a lower price.

## 4. Environmental Concerns

These are your basic environmental nightmares: radon, asbestos, and lead. Termites won't put you in the hospital, and can be discovered with a routine "termite inspection." Most environmental threats can also be easily detected, but determining what needs to be done about these problems will require some research. Make sure that your real estate contract includes contingency clauses in the event that certain environmental hazards are discovered.

### A. RADON

Radon is an odorless, colorless gas that occurs naturally and is found in certain types of rocky soil. Between five million and six million American homes are believed to have elevated radon levels. The Environmental Protection Agency (EPA) attributes 20,000 lung cancer deaths a year to the effects of radon.

While it's always hard to isolate one environmental contaminant as a cause of death, it clearly makes sense to test for the presence of radon in your home. Radon levels are easy to determine with an inexpensive do-it-yourself test kit ($10 to $25). Look for one that's approved by the EPA. What can be tricky is determining whether it's worth the high cost of constructing a ventilation system to eliminate the gas. If your test results indicate an elevated radon level in your home, consult the EPA for further instructions.

### B. ASBESTOS

Asbestos, commonly used through the late 1970s to insulate hot water pipes and as a fire retardant for radiators and boilers, is now known to be a cancer-causing substance. The American Medical Association (AMA), however, tells us that asbestos is only hazardous if it's actually crumpling or frayed, releasing particles into the air that can then be inhaled.

Make sure that your concerns about asbestos are dealt with prior to the closing and are in the final sales contract. Your contract should call on the seller to correct all asbestos problems on the premises, not just those found by your inspection.

Possible solutions for the presence of asbestos include encapsulating the asbestos, allowing it to remain sealed, or removing it all together. When my wife and I moved into our present home, we decided to have the asbestos in the basement wrapped, and not removed, since removal can cause large amounts of dangerous asbestos particles to be released into the air.

Whichever option you choose, make sure that you use

an asbestos company that's licensed by your state's department of environmental protection. The job will cost between $2,000 and $8,000, with most jobs at about $3,000.

C. LEAD

IN PAINT: Fact: Slums are not the only places where you'll find hazardous lead paint. According to the U.S. Department of Housing and Urban Development, 74% of homes built before 1980 contain potentially dangerous levels of lead and more than three million American children are believed to have dangerously high levels of lead in their blood. At higher levels, lead can cause toxic effects on the kidneys and nervous system, sometimes resulting in death. Even exposure to low levels of the poison has been linked to slowed intellectual development, reduced memory, and shortened attention spans.

What To Do: The federal government recommends that every child under the age of six be tested for lead—contact your child's pediatrician (cost of the blood test: about $30). If you believe your home may be at risk, get a building inspector to test for lead (cost: $50 to $150). There are also labs that can test paint samples from your home. Ask your local department of health for a referral. If you do have a problem, you'll need to contact a licensed contractor to remove the hazard (while you and your family flop at a relative's house for a few weeks).

IN WATER: Many homes have water pipes that are made of lead or are connected with lead solder. Some municipalities still have water mains and connecting lines made of lead. Also, some brass and chrome-plated faucets may contain lead. The effect: Lead poisoning can occur as a result of ingesting lead from your tap water.

What To Do: Contact the EPA or your state's department of environmental protection for a list of certified water-testing labs in your area. Cost of the test: $10 to $20 per sample. If you have a problem, consider switching to bottled water. Other, more expensive, options include filters approved by the National Sanitation Foundation or, as a last and very expensive resort, replacing your water pipes.

## 5. Buying Old Versus Buying New

The biggest problem with buying an old house is that few of us are Bob Vila. Many of us get stuck in the "I Can Fix It Myself Syndrome." Remember, it's hard to find the time, energy, or money to fix up a house after you move in. In the face of our many good intentions, there are regular jobs, demanding children, and all the other items of life that keep us more than busy.

Fix-up jobs usually get spread out over the course of many years. Make sure you're ready to live in an older home "as is" for a good period of time if the only way you can afford to make improvements is by doing the labor yourself. Always get professional estimates before you buy, just in case you have to call for help when you botch up a job or you continue to procrastinate for a decade or two.

## Single-Family Versus Multi-Family

### 1. Condos

The boom in condominiums was largely due to the great appreciation in land values experienced in many urban and suburban areas of the country during the 1970s and 1980s. A developer can squeeze more units, and more profit, into a set amount of land by building attached or multi-level condos. Condo prices tend to be less stable than those of single-family homes, primarily because their supply can increase much faster than that of single-family housing. In a boom, builders simply increase the density of condo developments by fitting more units into their building plans. The only factor regulating the density increase is the zoning laws of the municipality.

Condominium ownership means that you own your particular unit outright while you share ownership of the building's common areas like hallways, sidewalks, recreation and utility rooms. You'll have to pay your share of the expenses to keep these areas maintained. Check to see how stable this fee is. It's subject to whatever increases the elected condominium board decides to approve. Ask the condo's representatives for their assessment of future expenses. The board may be contemplating or delaying certain major repairs (expensive elevator work, a new oil burner, etc.) that could greatly affect your monthly charge.

Condominium politics can be intense. Ask about the

level of harmony and what issues the factions are fighting over at the present time. Shop around for an association that seems reasonable and efficient. Some are out of control.

*Advantage*: You're generally free to rent out your apartment to whomever you want. *Disadvantage*: Your neighbors can rent out their apartments to whomever they want.

## 2. Co-ops

In co-operative housing you live in a building owned by all the residents collectively. Your ownership interest is expressed as shares of stock in the corporation which owns the building. Along with your shares of stock you get the right to occupy your unit. Before you commit, get a feel for the level of harmony in a prospective building. Make sure there is a consensus about how much maintenance is to be performed.

*Disadvantage*: If you want to rent out your apartment you'll have to get the board's approval. *Advantage*: Since a portion of your monthly maintenance costs go toward paying the building's mortgage, you'll be able to deduct a certain percentage of these fees from your taxes. Check the building's prospectus for this percentage.

## Timeshares

The first rule about timeshares: Never take one of those company tours where you have to drive five hours to the property—even though you do get the chance to win a great prize and you are guaranteed to win something. It's like being taken prisoner. And when you don't buy, they might make your life difficult. What's more, your chances of winning a free car are practically nil, and the real prize you'll win is likely to be an assemble-it-yourself clock, worth a whopping $7.50 suggested retail.

There are two basic types of timeshares: deeded and non-deeded. Both give you the right to use a particular property, for a certain duration, at a specified time of the year. Obviously, Christmas week is going to cost you more than a week in mid-September.

In a deeded transaction, you actually have an ownership interest in a specific piece of property. In a non-deeded transaction, you are simply buying a lease or club membership that lets you vacation each year at a set time. Warning: Resale of timeshares can be hard, or next to impossible. Remember, you'll be going head-to-head with the crack sales force who talked you into the deal in the first place.

Make sure that you research timeshares very carefully since you're buying their good faith about promised maintenance, improvements, and other management responsibilities. Also, despite oral promises, the truth is that exchanges with other resorts are rarely guaranteed. As for sales practices, the timeshare industry ranks number one in high-pressure, close-em on the spot sales methods. Many people get seduced into buying timeshares while they're on vacation. Try not to make decisions of this sort when you're in the vacation-induced "life is wonderful" frame of mind.

Timeshares are usually regulated by each state's real estate commission. To obtain more information about timeshares, or to report deceptive practices, you can also contact the Federal Trade Commission, Division of Marketing Practices, 6th Street & Pennsylvania Avenue, N.W., Washington, D.C. 20580.

# Buying at Auction

Most real estate auctions require that you bid blindly and show that you're serious by forking over a down payment of about 10% of the purchase price. You then have thirty days to come up with the remainder of the final sale price. If you're not paying cash, and your mortgage plans fall through, you'll lose your down payment. Although you can visit a property prior to bidding on it, you probably won't have enough time for a complete evaluation by a professional inspector.

If you're thinking about buying at auction, be sure to attend several and follow the procedures carefully. If you're really serious about bidding, don't forget to bring an attorney. Bottom Line: Auctions are not for amateurs. The risk of not getting financing, and the difficulties involved in inspecting the property, make auctions extremely treacherous.

## Buying Investment Property

Being a landlord is not for everyone. Beyond that, the same skills in shopping for a property apply. The 1986 tax reforms, however, limited investors' access to certain write-offs and some experts argue that real estate took a major hit as a result. Whether it was tax reform, or just market forces which brought an end to real estate appreciation, the point is that real estate is a relatively high risk bet.

Many people try investing in real estate by taking out a new mortgage on their homes—sucking the down payment out of their home's equity. This strategy will usually only work if real estate values are rising much faster than the rate of inflation. You'll have to make your assessment based on the individual market or community you're speculating in. The fact that you won't be living in the property should free you to make a completely objective decision about where to buy.

## Contesting Your Property Taxes

You *can* fight city hall on this one. If you think you might be overpaying on your property taxes, call your municipality's tax assessor and ask to see a listing of the assessed values and taxes for other homes in your neighborhood. Look for homes that have approximately the same lot size, square footage, and year of construction. Also ask to see the worksheet ("property report card") for your home. This will show you exactly how the assessor calculated your home's taxes.

Ask the assessor what type of expert opinions are customary in fighting the valuation they've set for your home (but don't expect your town's assessor to be too cooperative in your efforts to reduce your payments). The point here is that there's a certain amount of judgment involved. All properties have unique aspects. You can also ask your local elected and appointed officials for advice. Their interest in getting reelected or reappointed makes tax assessments a real concern. Warning: Do your homework before you spend any money on a lawyer's consultations.

Contesting your property taxes can be a lengthy process. So be patient and try not to get too emotional. You may be able to save some REAL dollars in the end.

# THE REAL ROYAL SCAM

You're not going to believe this one! Some years ago, my wife and I were hanging out in our backyard when a young married couple—I didn't catch their last name—approached our house from their car, a nondescript blue station wagon if I remember correctly, and explained to us that they used to live in our house and could they please take a look to see how it had changed. We weren't aware of any major structural changes, but who could resist a former owner's request for one short look around?

As we talked outside, later, about the neighborhood and the neighbors who had left—we didn't recognize any of the names they mentioned—the wife asked if she could go back in and take just one more quick peek. "Why, of course!" we blabbered.

And as these nice strangers drove off (people with whom we now shared a strong common bond of having owned the same home) we waved good-bye, having no idea that we were also waving good-bye to some of my wife's favorite jewelry.

# Getting a Mortgage

### "Can I Qualify?
### What Am I Getting Myself Into?"

Getting a mortgage is a tricky process but one that can be successfully mastered with a little help from this book and your own self-confidence. Your ability to play hard and win at the mortgage game is critical to your financial health and well-being; for most of us, it will be by far our largest lifetime expense.

GOVERNMENT ACTION FORCED BANKERS TO "GET REAL"
In the old days, shopping for a mortgage was easy. You drove over to your local bank, spoke with your friendly neighborhood banker, filled out the application form, and chose from the few mortgage options he had to offer: usually basic vanilla or chocolate. In most areas, mortgages were only available from these local banks and a few upstart mortgage companies.

In an effort to loosen up this process, the federal government created a national system which encouraged lenders to provide money in all neighborhoods and all localities, assuring access to home ownership for everyone. The new system was born during the 1970s, and was then vastly expanded during the 1980s. In effect, two

government-sponsored corporations were formed to act
as clearinghouses for the local lenders. These agencies
became best known by their rather cute nicknames,
Fannie Mae (Federal National Mortgage Association)
and Freddie Mac (Federal Home Loan Mortgage Corp.).
The bottom line: Your mortgage lender gets the money
from Fannie or Freddie and then gives it to you.

THE NEW MORTGAGE DILEMMA: TOO MANY CHOICES
When you go out to shop for a mortgage today, you'll en-
counter a dizzying array of options. Today's mortgage
lenders offer a choice of options which reads like a menu
at a Chinese restaurant. Unless you're a mathematical ge-
nius, you'll probably need a calculator just to enter the
mortgage lender's office.

Typical Bank Slogan in 1970: "We've got the money
and you don't."

Typical Bank Slogan in 1994 (well, almost): "If we can't
get you the money in thirty minutes, your mortgage closing
costs are free—and you don't even have to pay us back."

WHAT'S CHANGED?
Today, the government-sponsored corporations "buy"
mortgages from lenders. More than half of new mortgages are "sold" to these so-called "secondary markets."
By selling mortgages to Freddie or Fannie, mortgage
companies are able to lend the same money again to
other borrowers. In case you're worried about it, your
lender does "quite well thank you" by selling off mort-

gages to the national markets and receiving commissions on each sale.

If a lender is feeling rich, it may not sell your mortgage right away. It even may want to gamble and keep your mortgage indefinitely. If interest rates drop, the value of your mortgage goes up, and the lender will be able to earn extra profit by selling your higher-interest-rate mortgage to another institution.

WHAT THE CHANGES MEAN TO YOU
Greater choice about where you can get a mortgage, but more red tape. Since most mortgages get sold, lenders must follow standards set by Freddie and Fannie. Lenders need to follow the rules and guidelines closely because failure to do so will make a mortgage loan unsaleable to these national mortgage clearinghouses.

## How to Shop for a Mortgage

### 1. Watch Out for Sales Pressure

Mortgages are sold by "mortgage originators" who will handle most of the details related to your new mortgage. They may also offer advice about which mortgage program is best for you. The problem here is that mortgage originators are paid on commission. They receive .5% to 1% (or more) of the loan amount for their efforts. Look out for biased advice which might encourage you to:

a) Borrow more than you need. It can be tempting to walk away from your mortgage closing with an extra $10,000 or $20,000 in your pocket. Borrow just what you need to purchase or refinance the property and not a penny more (unless you've planned certain specific home repair projects or want to use the extra money to pay off costly consumer loans).

b) Apply for a potentially risky adjustable rate mortgage, with a low starter rate, just so you can qualify for a loan.

c) Refinance when you really don't need to.

## 2. Get References

Check out the lender's business practices by calling your state's department of consumer protection or the office of the banking commissioner for your state, a special agency that deals solely with banking affairs and institutions. The names may change from state to state so use your phone book to get started with the process of learning your state's bureaucracy. Unfortunately, certain states are lagging behind in their policing of the mortgage industry.

Additionally, it's a good idea to inquire at your local branch of the Better Business Bureau. Make sure that they can do a computer data search outside your local area since many mortgage lenders operate nationally. Shy away from references given by organizations run by the mortgage lenders themselves: Foxes generally don't guard hen houses very well. For example, avoid outfits with names like the Mortgage Bankers Association of

America. They're likely to be much more interested in serving the needs of their members than in responding to your concerns as a consumer.

Also, if you're using a real estate agent, be alert to the fact that your agent is primarily concerned with seeing the sale go through as quickly as possible. Your agent may not care if you find a mortgage lender that saves you money. However, agents do see prospective lenders in action over time. Their evaluation of mortgage providers may be worth hearing. CAUTION: Ask your realtor if he or she has any formal or informal ties with the lenders they recommend. In some states, real estate companies are allowed to operate mortgage companies. If your realtor is getting an extra commission for referring you to a particular lender, take his or her advice with a very large grain of salt. Good News: Consumer advocates are working to limit such practices.

## How Much Can You Borrow?

### 1. Mortgage Qualification Rules

The 28%/36% rule of thumb is the key ratio. What this means is that the total of your mortgage payments (principal plus interest), property taxes, and homeowner's insurance must not exceed 28% of your gross (before tax) income.

Now for the 36% issue. All of your monthly bills, including what you'll be shelling out for your home, your car payments, student loans, boat payments, etc., must not exceed 36% of your gross income.

## 2. Down payments

You can't rely totally on generous relatives to get past this issue. Usually some of the down payment (around 3%) will have to come from your own savings. You're required to disclose the source(s) of your down payment, and remember that you'll be flirting with bank fraud if you get too tricky. Remember: The lender's concern is that you have a financial stake in the property. If a down payment is a problem for you, ask around as you shop. For every rule there are exceptions.

*Note:* If you put down less than 20%, you'll be required to obtain private mortgage insurance (PMI)—not very expensive.

## 3. Some Tricky Terms

The mortgage business has its own private language. We recommend that you try to get a handle on the following "buzzwords." Doing so will help you shop with greater confidence.

*Conventional mortgages:* These are the government-sponsored mortgages that are usually sold to entities like Freddie Mac and Fannie Mae. At present, the maximum size of these loans is around $190,000.

*Jumbo loans:* These are mortgages greater than about $190,000. Often, because of the higher amount involved, the interest rate is higher than that on Fannie Mae or

Freddie Mac conventional-size mortgages. The closing costs should be the same, except, of course, for those closing costs which are based on a percentage of the actual loan amount (points, etc.).

# Where to Shop for a Mortgage

Government action has provided access to a vast array of new lenders. As you check out the different types of mortgage lenders, remember not to judge a book by its cover. A bank might own a mortgage company which it may operate as a completely independent subsidiary. Also, a bank may simply be brokering your mortgage, collecting a commission for processing the loan. Options include:

## 1. Commercial Banks or Saving & Loans

PROS: They may have the nicest office furniture. They may have a branch location nearby. During the long application process, it's nice to have a convenient place to drop off all of the crazy documents they ask for.

CON: They often have higher interest rates than other lenders.

The problem with using the bank nearest to your home is price. If its prices are higher, then it's the same as buying your groceries for the next fifteen or thirty years at your local 7-Eleven. By signing on for a higher interest rate, you'll be overpaying for the duration of the loan.

## 2. Mortgage Companies

Mortgage companies are businesses that specialize in originating mortgages. They may or may not be actually providing the money.

PRO: They are very price-oriented and are generally very flexibile.

CON: They may not be for REAL. Some have been known to go out of business during the sixty or ninety days that it takes to close on a mortgage.

Check them out with your state and local consumer agencies.

---

### REAL TIP: BIGGER ISN'T NECESSARILY BETTER

You may be dealing with a company that has a staff of one person or a hierarchy of thousands. Again, checking references is advised. A small company may provide more attentive service, but there's a chance it may not know what it is doing. Large or small, look at the price of the mortgage as a whole. Getting references will allay your fears about the owner fleeing to Mexico with your application fee.

## 3. Mortgage Brokers

Mortgage brokers are basically loan matchmakers. These originators are usually favored by borrowers who are having trouble finding a loan through more traditional lenders. You should only play the mortgage broker game if you have one of the following problems:

A. *Credit history problems:* Before you turn over your problems to a mortgage broker, get a copy of your credit bureau report from at least one credit reporting company (TRW, Equifax, etc.) and check it for errors. If you find an error, you have the right to dispute the report or at least put your side of the story on the report.

B. *Trouble verifying earnings:* In order to qualify for a loan, you must detail your sources of income. For some, particularly those with income from a commissioned sales job, self-employment, or cash or off-the-books earnings, this can be a real hassle. But don't run to a mortgage broker until you've asked for a detailed explanation of income guidelines from a number of lenders.

C. *Unusual properties:* For example, your home has a bakery on the ground level or you operate a trailer park in your backyard. Traditional lenders generally shy away from "nonconforming" properties.

Brokers can also be helpful in sorting through the maze of mortgage choices available, and working to find a loan that makes sense for you. However, expect to pay extra money for their services.

A warning about a mortgage broker's fees: It's critical to establish the broker's fee up front. Make sure that they are really trying to find the best rate and terms for you. They may be more motivated by maintaining a close relationship with one or two specific mortgage companies or banks than by helping you find a good deal. DON'T PAY EXTRA FOR A BROKER UNLESS YOU'RE SURE IT'S ABSOLUTELY NECESSARY.

Also, never pay money to a broker up front. The mortgage broker's fee should be paid when, and only when, they get you the loan. However, once a broker has selected a specific lender, that lender may require payment for an appraisal of the property and/or an application fee of $200 to $300. Before you shell out your hard-earned cash, be sure to obtain, in writing, the broker's valuation of your chances of ultimately getting the mortgage through that source. Try to make the appraisal the last step in the application process. Most reputable lenders will provide you with an approval which is subject to the outcome of the appraisal.

## 4. Credit Unions

Check with your credit union about its home mortgage options and rates, if any. Remember though, just because a credit union services a limited membership, it may not be the cheapest source. Watch prices and rates carefully. Credit unions are trying to make a profit just like any other outfit.

## 5. Private Sources Including Relatives

Why not be creative. Suppose you know someone with the unfortunate problem of not knowing what to do with, say, an extra $100,000. Let's also say that this individual also wants to invest in something relatively secure. Other than government bonds, there aren't many low-risk investments that return as much as a mortgage loan with a stable borrower secured by a good home with a stable market value. Of course, if you don't pay, your relative-lender will have the right to foreclose on the mortgage and sell your home, just like any other lender.

### REALITY CHECK

Borrowing from a relative is relatively uncommon. How many of us have a rich aunt or uncle who is kind enough to lend us a quick $100,000, and ruthless enough to take our home away if we don't repay the loan? Make sure that your relationship can handle this worst-case scenario of foreclosure.

## 6. The Seller of the Property

These are called seller-financed, or seller take-back mortgages. The seller acts as a mortgage banker or lender and waits to receive the money from the sale over time, according to the terms of the mortgage loan contract.

PRO: The key advantage of seller take-back mortgages is that you avoid hassling with outside lenders, allowing greater flexibility for both the seller and the buyer.

CON: The seller could be nervous about collecting the monthly mortgage payments and may call you every thirty minutes on your scheduled payment day.

---

## REAL SCAM

Mortgages can be sold at a lender's discretion. My mortgage has been held by three different lenders in as many years. I learned not to take it personally after the second sale—it's only business I'm told, nothing personal. If your mortgage is sold, you should receive a "good-bye" letter from your existing lender at least fifteen days before the actual transfer of ownership. You will then receive payment instructions from your new lender.

Watch out for notices from phony mortgage companies instructing you to make all future payments to them at a certain address. By the time you realize what's happened, there could be a Chinese restaurant operating at that location. Only make payments to the company named in your lender's "good-bye" letter.

---

# Choosing a Mortgage That's Right for You

Now that you know where to shop for a mortgage, and the risks involved, you're ready to sort through the question of which type of mortgage is best for you.

## 1. Study the Mortgage Ads and Watch the Fine Print

As with car advertisements, many mortgage ads found in the newspaper, junk mail, and on television share one common problem for the consumer: They're all designed to get you into the lender's office. You may be able to get price information over the phone, but take these quotes with a grain of salt until you've actually gotten them in writing. Absolutely do not give up any money for an application or a property appraisal until you've been given the government-mandated disclosure forms, which itemize all costs.

## 2. Warm-Up Exercise:
## Don't Let Them Confuse You Over Costs
When shopping for a mortgage, keep an eye out for the different expenses:

- The actual interest rate itself.
- The loan's closing costs.
- The way the adjustable rate mortgage fluctuates, if you go that route.
- Penalties for early repayment.

## 3. The APR Game:
## The Government Tries to Play Umpire
In order to clamp down on lender-induced confusion, the federal government introduced the Annual Percentage Rate (APR) disclosure requirement. The APR is the "real" interest rate, taking into account the math involved in paying up-front costs and loan points. Always think in terms of the total amount you will have to pay over the life of the mortgage.

# Mortgages

## 1. Fixed-Rate Mortgages:
## For the Low-Risk Player

Fixed-rate mortgages are simple: The interest rate, and your monthly payments, are guaranteed for the life of the loan, usually fifteen or thirty years. Many borrowers choose fixed-rate mortgages because of the feeling of security they provide. If interest rates are relatively low, the security blanket of a fixed-rate loan is a fine idea. If rates drop in the future, you can always refinance. If they rise, you'll feel like a real Nobel Laureate for making such a wise choice.

---

### A REAL SMART MOVE:
### THE 15-YEAR MORTGAGE

No matter which type of mortgage you choose, you can probably get your lender to offer it over a 15-year term. The interest rate itself will be lower and you'll build up equity much faster.

PRO: Builds up your equity, the difference between what the property is worth and how much you owe, much faster than a 30-year loan.

EXAMPLE: AMOUNT OF LOAN BALANCE LEFT

|  | _15-year term_ | _30-year term_ |
|---|---|---|
| After 5 years: | 81% | 97% |
| After 10 years: | 49% | 91% |
| After 15 years: | 0 | 82% |

---

CON: The payments on a 15-year loan are approximately 20% to 25% higher. You'll have to be sure that you can consistently make the higher payment. Also, the mortgage lender may not allow you to choose the 15-year option if your payments will exceed approximately ⅓ of your after-tax income.

Option: You can simulate the advantage of a 15-year loan by paying an extra amount each month on your 30-year mortgage. This way, if you run into trouble down the road—lose your job, etc.—you'll have the option to withhold the extra amount. Ask your lender to prepare a plan for you.

## 2. Adjustable-Rate Mortgages: For the Gambler

Adjustable-rate mortgages offer interest rates which rise and fall in step with key interest rates or indexes. Each adjustable-rate mortgage contract specifies a particular index, which is chosen by the lender. Its purpose is to serve as an indicator of interest rate changes throughout the economy as a whole. By using an index, your lender is assured that you will be paying, over the life of the mortgage, approximately the same rate as any of its future borrowers.

*Pros:* If you feel rates are dropping, you can ride the wave, paying less each time your loan rate is adjusted. You also won't have to go to the trouble and expense of refinancing a fixed-rate mortgage if rates drop significantly. Adjustable-rate mortgages also carry lower initial rates than fixed-rate mortgages. *Note:* Adjustables are always a good idea if you know you're going to move within the next few years.

*Cons:* What goes down can also go up. You'll need to worry about your monthly payments increasing if interest rates go up. Make certain you deal with this uncertainty before you venture into an adjustable-rate mortgage.

A. THE MOST COMMON INTEREST RATE INDEXES

1. *The Treasury Bill (T-bill) Rate:* Treasury bills are short-term federal government IOU's. The one year T-bill is by far the most popular index used by first-mortgage lenders. However, two-, three-, and seven-year Treasury bonds and notes are widely utilized for mortgages that adjust every 2, 3, or 7 years, respectively. (Treasury bonds and notes have longer durations than T-bills.)

2. *The Prime Lending Rate:* This is the average rate banks across the country charge for loans to established businesses with excellent credit histories.

B. HOW ADJUSTABLE-RATE INDEXES WORK
If a mortgage is indexed to the prime rate, for example, a mortgage lender checks that rate when the loan is scheduled to be adjusted and adds on 2%, 3%, or whatever "margin" over the prime is specified in your contract.

C. THE INS AND OUTS OF CAPS
Caps give you some additional security if rates rise quickly. In the case of one-year adjustables, for example,

there is usually a cap which limits interest rate increases to 2% each year—your mortgage rate cannot rise by more than 2% each time it comes up for an adjustment. Lifetime caps place a limit on the total amount the interest rate can go up (usually about 6%) over the entire life of your mortgage, no matter how much the index rises.

### D. LOOK OUT FOR TEASER RATES

Here's where a lot of abuse occurs. Mortgage ads try to pull you into the lender's office by using "teaser rates," particularly on adjustable-rate mortgages. Those "too good to be true" numbers are usually valid for the first year or two. After that, the rate floats, and the loan usually ends up costing you more, after a few years, than today's going rate on a fixed-rate mortgage.

## REAL WARNING

Make sure you check the lender's math at each adjustment interval. In an alarming number of cases, there have been significant mistakes made when calculating the new monthly payment—usually in the lender's favor.

## 3. Two-Step Mortgages

A hybrid of fixed-rate and adjustable-rate loans, the interest rate on these mortgages starts at a slightly lower-than-market rate and then goes up after a period of time, usually five or seven years, to a higher interest rate, which then remains fixed for the remainder of the loan. The "you can't get a free lunch" principle certainly applies here. You may enjoy slightly lower payments during the starter period, but you will make up for it with higher closing costs and higher rates during the second stage of the loan. In general, step-mortgages end up costing you more in the long run than more straightforward fixed-rate and adjustable-rate mortgages.

## 4. Bi-Weekly Mortgages

Bi-weekly mortgages offer another way to shorten your repayment term and build equity faster. As the name suggests, you make mortgage payments, equal to one half your normal monthly payment, every two weeks. Result: You end up making the equivalent of one extra payment, or about 8% extra, every year. *Advantage:* A 30-year mortgage can be repaid in about nineteen years, saving you thousands of dollars in interest.

## 5. Reverse Mortgages

Growing in popularity in recent years, reverse mortgages are typically utilized by older individuals who have already finished paying for their homes and want to get money out of their property to pay for living expenses or some other use without having to move. Under this scenario, the lender issues monthly checks to the property owner and/or establishes a credit line against which the owner can borrow, and keeps a running tab of how much is paid out. When the property is finally sold, the lender gets these payments back, plus interest and closing costs.

The biggest advantage of this program is that it allows

an elderly person or couple to remain in their home as they age. Disadvantages include high interest rates and fees, and a reduction of your hard-earned equity. You may also be seduced into staying in a home that you really can't afford.

## 6. Government Subsidized Mortgages

These are likely to be the best deal in town, especially those offered by certain state programs that are designed to help lower- and middle-income borrowers purchase their first home. Subsidized mortgages are available through banks, mortgage companies, and other lenders that sell regular mortgages.

To see if you qualify for a state sponsored mortgage, simply call your state government's housing authority. Given the high cost of housing, you shouldn't feel guilty about using a subsidized program. It's not welfare—it's strictly allocated on the basis of total family income. The emphasis here is on helping the middle class family, squeezed out of their local housing market due to the high cost of real estate, achieve home ownership.

## 7. VA/FHA Mortgages

1. *VA: Veteran's Administration mortgages.* Available if you or your spouse served twelve months or more in a branch of the service. These mortgages require a small or, in many cases, no down payment, and usually offer a slightly lower than market interest rate. Offered through banks and mortgage companies, the government insures

the lender in the case of a foreclosure. To see if you qualify, contact the Veterans Administration at 202-872-1151.

2. *FHA: Federal Housing Authority mortgages.* These mortgages are great if you're only able to make a small down payment, even less than 5%. Again, the government insures the loan. Problem: Loans may not exceed $125,000, less in areas where home prices are lower than the national average. For more information, contact the FHA, 451 7th Street S.W., Washington, D.C. 20410.

---

# The Second Mortgage/ Home Equity Loan Game

---

*Second mortgages* are additional mortgages which provide you with cash from the equity in your home and give your lender the right to foreclose if you miss your payments. Second mortgages usually carry a fixed rate of interest and can run anywhere from five to fifteen years.

*Home equity* lines of credit are another, more popular, type of second mortgage that allows you to write checks against your home's equity, using the money when and how you choose. *Advantage:* You pay interest only on the amount you are actually using. Also, interest rates and payback terms can be more flexible than with traditional second mortgages. *Disadvantage:* Your closing costs will probably be higher than with a second mortgage and you'll have to be very disciplined not to use your credit line like a regular checking account.

## Use Second Mortgages Wisely

Being too loose with refinancing can get you into REAL trouble. When you borrow money against your home, you'll be paying the money back over a rather long time frame, typically ten to fifteen years. If you use money from your home's equity for a recurring expense, like new cars—look out! You'll end up paying interest on the loans long after the goods they've paid for have passed beyond their useful life.

Remember, you're risking your hard-earned equity. Only take out a second mortgage if you really need the money—to pay for a child's college tuition, make needed home improvements, etc. To protect yourself, don't take out a loan for more than you actually need.

*Should I borrow against my home to buy a car or pay off consumer debts?* The answer to this question depends on many factors. Naturally, don't risk your home to fund a shopping spree or buy a fancy new car. If you really need to buy a car, however, it may be cheaper to use a second mortgage if:

1. You already have a home equity line of credit and don't have to pay for the loan's closing costs and fees.
2. You can't find a cheap auto loan. Remember, the interest on the first $100,000 of your home equity loan is tax-deductible, while consumer loans now offer no tax advantage. Try to find a short-term loan, running four or five years, so you don't end up paying

a lot of interest. You'll also have to be very disciplined. You're borrowing against your home to
avoid, or pay off, consumer debts. If you take on a
second mortgage to pay off your credit cards, and
then simply take on more consumer debt in the future, you've accomplished nothing. Make sure that
you're able to fend off any temptation to spend your
precious equity line on frivolous pursuits.

### REAL CAUTION

When shopping for a second, or home equity, mortgage,
be aware that the APR on these loans does not reflect the
closing costs and other fees and charges the way it does
on a first mortgage. You'll have to compare each of these
costs, and the interest rates, among several different
lenders.

## How to Tackle The Closing Cost Game

### 1. Keep Your Eyes Wide Open

You'll need to keep track of a whole laundry list of small
closing costs in order to keep your lender honest. Always
see if anything is negotiable.

## REAL WARNING:
## CHECK THE FINE PRINT

The U.S. government, in an effort to protect consumers from getting ripped off by unscrupulous lenders, mandated that all first mortgage lenders must follow specific procedures during the application process. These procedures are dictated by the federal truth-in-lending laws. Lenders are required to provide you with a form called a "Good Faith Estimate Of Closing Costs," which details your loan's closing costs. Beware: These forms often have errors; you must check each item carefully.

## 2. Get to Know What Points Are About

Points are mortgage origination fees. Each point is equal to 1% of the amount you borrow. If you're refinancing, the points can be "rolled into" your loan amount. In plain English, you'll be borrowing the points along with the money you're actually getting from the loan. If it's a first mortgage for the purchase of a property, you'll have to shell out the points from your own pocket at the time of the closing.

### POINTS VERSUS THE INTEREST RATE

Don't get fooled. If your loan has points, your interest rate should be lower. As a general rule of thumb, paying one point (1% of the amount you borrow) should reduce your interest rate by about .125%—what a banker calls 12½ basis points.

POINTS AND YOUR INCOME TAXES

It's important to check with your accountant regarding the deductibility of points on your income taxes. Currently, points are tax-deductible on your next return if you're buying a house for the first time or, in the case of a second mortgage, you're using the money for home improvements. If you're refinancing, you can only deduct the points over the life of the loan. In other words, if you're getting a 30-year mortgage, you can only deduct ⅟₃₀ of the cost of the points in each of the next thirty years.

## 3. The Closing Costs Package

On average, expect to spend about 2% of your loan amount (excluding "mortgage origination fees" or points—see above) on closing costs, which include:

- *The application fee.* Covers the lender's initial cost of processing your loan request. It's generally non-refundable ($200 to $350).
- *The appraisal fee.* Pays for an independent appraisal of the property. It's required before a loan can be approved ($250 to $400). May be included in your application fee.
- *Property survey.* Insures that the property actually exists as it's stated on the deed. My wife and I were fortunate enough to avoid this fee because our lender accepted an existing survey of our property ($125 to $400).
- *The lender's lawyer's fee.* It doesn't seem fair that you should have to pay for the other side's legal costs

when they're working to create a document which will make them money and cost you thousands in mortgage interest. But that's the way it is. In a soft market, a lender may cut you some slack on these expenses, but make sure that they're not simply jacking up the interest rate a bit to make up the difference. One lender I spoke with was demanding a lawyer's fee of $900. The lawyer they use, not coincidentally, also owned the mortgage company ($350 to $900).

- *Title search and title insurance.* The purpose of this search at the town's hall of records is to make sure that the seller isn't merely pretending to own the house, and, to get a history of the property. For their own protection, mortgage lenders accept nothing on its face value and, in this case, require that *you* pay for an insurance policy that covers the loan amount in the event that you buy a home from someone other than the rightful owner ($450 to $900).
- *Recording fees.* The cost for filing the mortgage at the local registry of deeds or hall of records. It's usually a small item. ($40 to $65).
- *Credit bureau reports.* Should be free, but they bleed you over this. Try to negotiate this one off your tab ($35 to $50).
- *Anything else they can sneak into the forms.* Don't feel bad if they do it to you, they usually make a practice of it. Always clarify the expenses, item by item, and don't be afraid to ask questions.

WARNING: Don't get burned on closing costs for a second or home equity mortgage—they should cost much less than a typical first mortgage since you probably won't need a new title search, survey, etc.

## 4. Other Closing Cost Issues

### A. LOCK-INS

Allow you to secure a lender's interest rate quote for a specific period of time, usually thirty or sixty days. Lock-ins give you security while your application is processed. A lender may charge extra for extending the lock-in period but you may be able to find a lender who will give you the lowest rate that becomes available during the lock-in period you choose. More commonly, a lender will only allow you the one-time option to lock in your rate at anytime during the lock-in term, giving you the chance to play interest-rate gambler. Whatever lock-in option you choose, get it in writing.

### B. PMI (PRIVATE MORTGAGE INSURANCE)

Actually means you'll have to be approved twice, by the mortgage lender and the private mortgage insurer. The company insures the amount you borrow over 80% of the property's value. If you make a 20% down payment, PMI isn't required. Be aware that you'll be paying a set amount each month for this insurance. Make sure that you can get out of paying for PMI when your equity equals 20% of the property's value, either as a result of your monthly payments or the property's market appreciation. The smaller your down payment, the higher your PMI costs.

### C. ESCROW ACCOUNTS

Another area of abuse. Congress is now working to eliminate "escrow shock" or "escrow padding." Escrow funds are monies, YOUR MONIES, that are set aside by the lender to maintain control over the flow of payments for property taxes and homeowner's insurance. In many cases, lenders are setting aside TOO MUCH OF YOUR MONEY in these accounts. Why? Because lenders are only required to pay a very low rate of interest on escrow accounts (usually about 2%). In many states, they aren't required to pay any interest at all! They can invest YOUR money at competitive rates and enjoy the spread.

To protect yourself against escrow padding, ask for a printout of your daily balance for the previous year. As a general rule, unless your contract allows for it, your lowest balance should be no more than twice your monthly escrow payment.

My wife and I were lucky enough to negotiate our way out of this onerous requirement and we now pay directly our own insurance bills and property taxes. In some states, you may be required to make a larger down payment before you can negotiate this point. Ask your lender what it takes to get an escrow-release. They may tell you that it's impossible—it's not!

D. PREPAYMENT PENALTIES

These are monies you'll owe if you pay your mortgage off early, either through the sale of the property or refinancing. WARNING: Check your contract carefully. Prepayment penalties can clobber you, forcing you to pay a ton of money if you leave your mortgage early.

E. NEGATIVE AMORTIZATION

Not only does this concept sound dangerous, it actually is. If interest rates rise rapidly, your adjustable-rate mortgage payments may not adequately cover your lender's real costs. In this case, if your contract allows for negative amortization, your lender has the right to get THEIR "lost" money out of the equity in YOUR property causing your loan amount to grow like the national debt. Be sure to avoid this provision at all costs.

## The Refinancing Game

The traditional rule of thumb says to refinance your mortgage when interest rates drop more than 2% below your existing rate. You'll have to consider the closing costs when you make your calculations. Usually it will take at least three years before, in the final tally, you really save money by refinancing. If you're thinking about moving in the next few years, it probably only pays to refinance if you use a short-term adjustable-rate mortgage.

When shopping for a new mortgage, always start with

your existing lender. It may be willing to restructure or modify your existing loan, saving you big money on closing costs.

## Under What Circumstances Should You Refinance?

- You want to take advantage of lower rates.
- You are tired of the uncertainty of an adjustable-rate mortgage and want to switch to a predictable fixed-rate loan.
- You want to switch to an adjustable-rate mortgage with better terms (rate and caps) than your existing ARM.
- You want to convert to a shorter-term loan, building equity faster.
- You want to increase your loan amount to make use of the equity in your home to pay for a major expense—college tuition, etc.

### REAL CAUTION

With property values *declining* in certain areas of the country, you may not be able to refinance your mortgage for as much as you would like. Why? The underlying "loan to value" ratio (LTV) may have changed, making you ineligible to borrow your original loan amount. Only an appraisal will determine what your property is worth today. If you've suffered a loss in market value, you may have to borrow less (paying off some of the original loan with your own money), delay your plans for refinancing, or get PMI.

# Losing the Game:
# Coping With a Foreclosure

Foreclosure proceedings don't usually start until at least ninety days after you stop paying your bills. Until that time, a lender, like any other bill collector, will usually just send nasty collection letters. If you do get into trouble, notify your lender as soon as possible. You may be able to buy an extra month or two. Hiding from the truth won't make it any less true or painful.

## Getting Money Back After a Foreclosure

Should you be unfortunate enough to have your property foreclosed on by a lender, you are entitled to the difference between what you owed on your mortgage(s) and what the forced sale or auction sale generates. With the bank's legal fees and late charges tacked on, however, the recent buyer, who put up only a modest down payment, has only a slim chance of getting any money back—sort of like the chances of becoming one of those "no-fail, no-money down" real estate millionaires featured on late night television.

## REAL PROTECTION—ESTABLISH A FORECLOSURE RESERVE FUND:

Many borrowers overextended themselves during the 1980s. Thinking that real estate prices, and their own personal fortunes, would perpetually rise, many of these borrowers have now run into trouble. And with many couples relying on two incomes to make ends meet, a loss of one job could make it difficult to make monthly mortgage payments.

For these reasons, it's very important to establish a reserve fund to cover any sudden job loss or reversal of fortune, particularly in this age of diminishing job security. Experts traditionally advised keeping at least 3 months of expenses on hand. More of these experts are today recommending at least a 6-month reserve.

## Keep the Faith

The one thing to remember about mortgages is that, one way or another, you're going to have to pay one. Even if you're a renter, you're still paying a mortgage—your landlord's.

# 4  $ 🏠 🚗 🎓 ♥

# Insurance and Planning Ahead

### "If It's Not Already Too Late"

**D**eath. Disease. Disability. None of us expect these things to happen to us or our loved ones any time soon, but they can and often do. On an average day in the United States, 261 Americans die in accidents while another 22,740 of us suffer serious work-related injuries. Also on an average day, 2,433 of our cars are stolen and 3,474 of our homes are lost or severely damaged in fires. In all, accidents cost Americans $323,287,671 in damages each and every day.

So is there an answer for these terrible uncertainties of life? Yes, well sort of anyway, insurance. Besides prayer, insurance is the only answer most of us have for life's terrible and random events. And while bad things may happen to us anyway, we can, through insurance, make certain that we have the ability to support our survivors, pay our hospital bills, or repair our damaged homes and cars. This chapter is a guide through the sometimes gruesome subject of insuring our lives and property.

And remember, it CAN happen to you.

# Life Insurance: Buy Some "Art"

With death being the only sure thing in life (taxes aren't even certain anymore), you'd think that life insurance would be a very big business. Well, you'd be dead right. *Ooops!* I mean you'd be completely accurate. In 1990, the most recent year reported, Americans were covered by life insurance policies worth a whopping $9.4 trillion. That comes to more than $37,000 for every man, woman, and child in the country. In that same year, more than $76 billion in premiums were paid on those policies to the nation's 2,200 life insurers. In turn, these insurers paid out $24 billion in death benefits.

These are large dollars. But the average Biff and Tiffany probably spend more time researching the relative merits of a new stereo system than their purchase of a life insurance policy. And who can blame them? Death is a pretty distasteful subject. And thanks to the insurance companies, life insurance products are hopelessly complex. Would you like a whole life, universal life or indeterminate premium whole life policy? How about a ten-year reentry term policy? Are you asleep yet? I said "ARE YOU ASLEEP YET!"

Luckily, you can sidestep all of these headaches with a few key rules that boil down to just one basic principle: Buy *ART*. No, not the stuff that hangs in museums, *A*nnual *R*enewable *T*erm insurance.

## 1. Do One Thing And Do It Right

To hear your friendly neighborhood insurance agent tell it, life insurance policies can do everything short of cooking your Sunday brunch. They can finance your retirement, pay for college tuition, provide you with easy loans and lucrative investments, and even pay your taxes. The claims can sound more like the rantings of a television infomercial than a regulated commodity.

While the claims may or may not be true, they have nothing to do with the main goal of life insurance, to provide income protection to your family in the event you check out early from the game of life. Life insurance helps your loved ones—and even those you just feel responsible for—carry on financially after you've gone. When insurers add other goals to life insurance policies, they collide with one of our cardinal rules: If you try to do more than one thing at the same time, you'll end up doing nothing well.

---

### REAL-LIFE TIP

BAD BENEFICIARY DESIGNATION: "To my son Patrick."
*BETTER BENEFICIARY DESIGNATION:* "Divided equally among all of my children."

REASON: If you have another child after you buy your policy, you may forget to add him or her as a beneficiary. The "to my children" type of designation solves that problem.

## 2. Get "Term" Not "Perm"

You may ask, "What does doing one thing well have to do with the overwhelming variety of life insurance policies?" Mainly, it means you can ignore most of the options.

Life insurance comes in two basic types, term and permanent (also called cash value). Term insurance provides you with pure income protection. You pay a premium based on your age, sex, weight, smoking habits, etc., and if you die while the policy is in force your designated beneficiaries receive $100,000, $250,000, or whatever the policy's death benefit is. You have no equity in the policy. It only has value if you die. (So, why not call it death insurance?—must have been a marketing decision!)

Permanent insurance, on the other hand, yields a cash value, or equity. You accumulate a balance over time that you can then withdraw as needed, or borrow against. Of course, doing so reduces your policy's death benefit.

You pay for this cash value feature. For example, a 35-year old male might buy a $100,000 term policy for just $140 a year, while a comparable permanent policy would cost nearly $1,000. Another difference between term and "perm": Term premiums rise as one ages (though there are level-premium varieties), while premiums for permanent insurance usually remain fairly constant because the interest on your cash accumulation goes toward paying the premium.

Permanent insurance goes by a parade of names: whole life, universal life, etc. Permanent insurance is the type that agents most often hawk for every goal from taxes to tuition. Experts say that such insurance can be useful. Some people, for example, may like its tax advantages. It can also be a wise choice if you'll need to worry about the tax impact of a large estate.

Permanent policies may also be useful as part of a forced savings plan for those of us who have trouble saving. But high agent commissions and the one-thing-at-a-time rule lead most consumer advocates to advise going with "term" not "perm."

## SHOPPING TIP

If you do decide to go with permanent insurance, make sure that the projections of future returns are based on historical data and not unsubstantiated estimates. Insurers often inflate their expectations of future interest rates and minimize their estimates of future company expenses. Compare the *guaranteed rates*—those rates that are set by law. Best bet: Look at the relative past performance of your selected companies.

### 3. Stop! Do You Really Need a Piece of The Rock?

With all due respect, an agent who says you don't need insurance is as rare as a tobacco industry executive who acknowledges the dangers of second-hand smoke. After all, they're paid by commission (that's why they push permanent policies so hard—the commissions are five to ten times higher than with term because of the higher amounts involved). So chances are you're the only one who will be able to figure out if you don't need insurance.

Fortunately, it's not that hard to do. We know that the aim of life insurance is income protection. This means that the sole employed parent in a family with young children is a clear candidate for a policy. Without insurance, the family would flounder if it were to lose that person's income.

By similar reasoning, the following people usually don't need any life insurance:

- Children
- Single persons having no dependents
- DINKS (young married couples with *Double Income* and *No Kids*)

### REAL-LIFE TIP

With AIDS and the health-cost crisis upon us, some insurers are offering life insurance policies with an accelerated death benefit. What this means is that you can collect your death benefit before you die in order to pay for medical costs, nursing home costs, etc.

### 4. ART Is Smart

Okay. Term insurance is what you want but what kind of term is the best? The answer is, as previously stated, *An*nual *R*enewable *T*erm. The policy is annual because its coverage extends for just one year. ART is renewable because, even though it expires at the end of a year, it can be renewed by payment of the next year's premium without an additional medical questionnaire or one of those obnoxious physical exams. A healthy 35-year-old man (or woman) can start an ART policy, submit to the initial medical exam, and then continue his or her policy without any further medical tests or inquiries as he or she ages, and his or her health inevitably declines. All you have to do is make your payments on time.

In this way, ART has a leg up on another variety of term known as reentry term. While these policies can sometimes be cheaper than term, the problem lies in the word "reentry." Every one, five, or even ten years, a "reentry" policyholder must submit to another medical exam. If his or her health has declined, the premiums will skyrocket.

The right to renew ART policies is limited to age 65 or 70. That's not so bad. Usually, your life insurance needs diminish as you age. In your retirement years, there will be no large income to protect and your kids will be out of school and on their own—or so you hope. Term premiums are prohibitively expensive after age 65 anyway. But, for those wishing or needing to continue life insurance into their golden years, many term policies are convertible to the permanent, cash value variety without a medical examination.

### REAL-LIFE TIP

Insurers often count your age from your nearest birthday, which may be your next one, not your last one. Strategy: Lock in a lower premium by buying within six months of your last birthday.

## 5. Count It Up

Okay boys and girls, It's Math Time! No, don't run—it's not that bad—I'll help you! Here's the $64,000 question: How much ART do you need to support your spouse and kids well into the next century? $50,000? $250,000? $500,000? $1,000,000? Unfortunately, you can't whip out a calculator for this one. You'd need a rather powerful computer to do it right, factoring in tuition cost trends, expected inflation, tax rates, the expected price of Häagen-Dazs bars, and so on. Since that's probably a mission impossible, you have these choices:

### A. "FIVE TIMES YOUR INCOME"

A common rule of thumb says that your life insurance benefit should equal five times your annual before-tax (gross) income. This rule assumes that the insured is the breadwinner in a family with young children. It's a good rough estimate, though some now say that, in light of lower interest rates, seven times income is better.

### B. FILL IN THE BLANKS

Some people may want to customize the calculation of their insurance needs rather than rely on a ballpark rule. For them, various worksheets are available from *Consumer Reports*, the American Council of Life Insurance, and others. Insurance agents should be able to help too. But you'll need to do most of the work yourself, figuring in such numbers as your mortgage, car loan, baby-sitting budget, pension benefits, and more, to get an accurate personalized estimate of your needs.

*Beware:* Don't buy and forget! Additional children, high inflation, and other changes can boost your insurance requirements. Make a point to review your policy at least once every two years.

---

### REAL-LIFE TIP

When calculating your insurance needs, be sure to subtract the value of any group life policies you have through work and any liquid assets you may have.

---

## 6. Time to Shop

Fine. You know what kind of life insurance you want and how much of it you need. But which of the country's 2,200 life insurance companies has the best buy for you? The task basically involves comparison-shopping. Here's what to do:

### A. FIND LOW RATES

Insurers set premiums by age, sex, health history, smoking habits, and a few other factors. Another pattern: The bigger the policy the lower the price ("rate") per thousand dollars of insurance. Beyond this, things are less predictable. Some insurers may have bargains in smaller ART policies, some in larger ones. Some have attractive rates early in a policy, some charge improved rates in later years. To compare them all you'd need to employ an accounting firm.

Luckily, there are ways to cut to the chase in this

drama. One is to contact the National Insurance Consumer Organization (703-549-8050) and ask for a copy of *Taking the Bite Out of Insurance* ($13.95 plus shipping and handling), which charts benchmark ART rates and recommends specific insurers. Two good rate-shopping services available at no or low cost are SelectQuote (800-343-1985), which will send you the five cheapest available policies for a person of your age, sex, and health; and Independent Advantage Financial and Insurance Services (800-829-2887), which provides a comparable listing service. Both services screen insurers for financial stability too—a growing concern during these uncertain economic times.

---

### REAL-LIFE TIP

Most life insurance is sold through commission-paid agents and brokers. However, some savings banks and insurers—USAA Life of San Antonio is one example—sell ART policies using their own salaried employees. Using these companies can often help you avoid higher prices and high-pressured sales pitches. If you do use an agent or broker, scrutinize his or her experience and training. It's a plus if he or she is a Chartered Life Insurance Underwriter (CLU).

---

B. SEEK SERVICE TOO

Low rates aren't the last word in insurance. Service counts too. Ask friends and relatives about the reputations of the companies you're considering. Also check with your state insurance department—the primary regulators of the industry—for a report on each company's record.


C. BEWARE THE BUST

The real estate bust that shattered the S&L industry also bruised some life insurers, with many of them taken over or resuscitated by state regulators. Most life insurers are healthy, however, and if you buy term insurance you're at less risk than with cash value policies. But, if your insurer goes belly up your money may be in danger; government protections in insurance are weaker than in banking where customers can rely on federal government deposit insurance (FDIC). So before you sign on the dotted line, verify your company's financial stability:

1. *Consult a service which gauges the financial strength of insurance companies and choose only the most highly rated.* The standard services are A.M. Best, Moody's, and Standard & Poor's. Their reports should be available in any larger library. Confine your candidates to insurers rated at least *A* by Best, *Aa* by Moody's, and *AA* by Standard & Poor's. But don't rely solely on these reports. Many insurance raters have been under fire for their allegedly too-cozy relationships with the industry and too-generous evaluations.

A new rater, Weiss Research Inc, is a for-profit consumer advocacy agency that is thought by many to be a tougher evaluator than the other three. Weiss ratings may be somewhat harder to find but you can order them through the company by calling 800-289-9222 (cost: $15 per rating). You may also find them listed in newspapers from time to time.

2. *Ask your insurance broker or agent about the company's risky-asset rate.* This number compares potentially bad outstanding loans with the firm's financial cushion. If it's 100%, or close, be careful!

---

## REAL-COMMON PROBLEM: "I FORGOT TO PAY THE PREMIUM"

Don't panic. State law usually gives you a thirty-day grace period to pay premiums without any penalty. Most insurers give you another thirty days to reinstate your policy without another health exam.

TIP: Pay premiums annually. It'll cost you less than monthly or quarterly payments, and you'll be less likely to forget to pay.

---

## 7. Sign on the Dotted Line

Okay. It's nearly over—except for paying your policy's premiums. Before you sign, here are some crucial tips for deciding on the exact specifications of your policy:

### A. PASS UP THE "RIDERS"

Riders are extras on your basic insurance policy. One applies a cost-of-living adjustment, so your policy keeps pace with inflation. The accidental death benefit—the famed "double indemnity" clause—pays your beneficiary a bonus if you die in an accident (for example, you are

killed by lightning while watching a golf tournament).
While such riders may be worthwhile in some circumstances (the waiver of premium provision if you become
disabled is a good idea), the prevailing word is to pass
them up. They cost too much and you get too little.


## B. BE HONEST!

To get coverage, you will have to supply information
about your health and, perhaps, submit to a medical examination. Now everyone may know you've been trying
to stop smoking and that you only smoke ultra-lights
anyway, but don't be tempted to answer questions
falsely in a quest for lower premiums. False information
can jeopardize your coverage. Most life insurance policies have a two-year contestability provision. If you
should die within two years from the start date of your
policy, your insurer has the right to review all information you have provided and void the claim if they find
any misrepresentations. But cheer up! If you finally do
toss your ultra-lights into the trash—not lighted,
please!—let your insurer know. You'll get your premiums reduced.


## C. TELL YOUR BENEFICIARY

All your good work may be wasted if you don't let your
beneficiaries know that the policy exists. Many policies
go uncollected because the insured never told his or her
loved ones about the coverage. Provide your beneficiaries

with a copy of the policy with instructions and relevant phone numbers.

# Disability Insurance: Illness and Injury

You contract a disabling disease. You sustain a hobbling injury. Maybe the disability is permanent, or maybe you'll be back on your feet in a year. Your health insurance will take care of the medical bills, but what about your income? You can't do your old job, or maybe even any job.

Providing such income protection is the aim of disability insurance. You may ask, "Does a healthy young person like me need disability-income insurance?" The answer is yes. In fact, you need it more than you need life insurance. One reason: In the thirty-five-to-sixty-five-year-old bracket your chances of disability are six times greater than your chances of death. Another reason: Disability can put your family in a greater financial fix than your death, because with disability your personal expenditures—perhaps including big medical bills—continue.

## 1. A Puzzle of Policies

Here's the good news: You may already have disability-income insurance. There is a patchwork of public and private sources, and understanding them is the key to figuring out if you need more. The two biggest sources of disability insurance are Social Security and group policies at the workplace:

## A. SOCIAL SECURITY

If you're eligible for Social Security retirement benefits you are eligible for disability benefits, too. In 1989, 4.1 million Americans received nearly $29 billion in such payments. How much you get depends on your income and your time under Social Security coverage. These benefits are the most significant part of Social Security for younger workers, but they have strict eligibility rules:

- Your disability must be expected to last at least a year and result in death.
- Monthly payments don't begin until six months after the onset of your disability.
- Most important, "disability" is strictly defined as the inability to perform *any* gainful employment—not just your customary occupation. If, for example, a dentist is disabled but can still stuff envelopes, he or she is ineligible for Social Security disability benefits.

## B. ON THE JOB

"Sick days" for which you are paid are a form of disability-income benefit offered by many employers. Also, some states require employers to furnish workers with short-term disability benefits. New Jersey and New York, for instance, require businesses to pay for at least twenty-six weeks of such benefits. In more employee-friendly California, it's fifty-two weeks.

Although there are no federal or state laws regarding long-term disability benefits, surveys have found that nearly half of the nation's medium and large enterprises do offer policies to their workers. These policies cover between 30% and 40% of the working population—so your chances of having such coverage are pretty good.

Employers pay for many of these disability policies, which replace an average 60% of a worker's predisability salary. Beyond that, though, the policies vary. Payments can last anywhere from five years to life. Some policies begin payments immediately upon disability, others have waiting periods of six months or more. To get a fix on the terms of your workplace disability policy, talk to your benefits officer. He or she can also help you determine your Social Security coverage.

## TAX TIP

Disability payments from employer-paid policies are taxable. But, if you pay for your own coverage, the benefits are tax-free.

There are many other sources of disability-income insurance. Here are some of the other pieces to the puzzle:

- *Workers' compensation.* If your illness or injury is job-related, you may be eligible for workers' compensation benefits.

- *Civil service.* Government workers often have excellent disability benefits.
- *Military service.* Contact the Veterans Administration about pension disability benefits.
- *Auto insurance.* Some car policies provide payments for disabilities resulting from auto accidents.
- *Unions.* Some unions furnish disability benefits to their members.

## 2. Individual Coverage: Fill in the Gaps

Okay. The picture is emerging, but some pieces are still missing. Perhaps you have a pretty good disability policy at work but the payment period is only ten years. And you do have Social Security coverage—but you know that it only applies to devastating disabilities.

You can fill in these gaps with an individual policy. As with all insurance policies, there are many major issues:

### A. DISABILITY DEFINED? BROADLY

This is the most crucial aspect of disability insurance. Make sure the policy covers disabilities due to either illness or accident; some policies only protect against the latter. Also select a policy that takes effect when you become unable to perform your customary job—not any possible job.

### B. PARTIAL DISABILITY? TOTAL DISABILITY?—BOTH

Opt for a policy that covers both partial and total disabilities.

## C. WAITING PERIOD? LONG

This is the time between the onset of your disability and the start of your benefits. Some policies offer immediate payments, but to keep your premiums down choose a six-month wait or more.

## D. PAYMENT PERIOD? UNTIL AGE 65

This aspect of the policy is not the place to save on premiums. Disability insurance protects your income from catastrophic illness or injury. A ten-year benefits-payment-period won't do the job if you are permanently disabled at age thirty. Opt for benefits that continue until normal retirement age.

## E. BENEFIT SIZE? REASONABLE

To discourage malingerers, aka deadbeats, insurers limit benefits to about 70% of your pre-tax salary. Ask insurers for worksheets to help you calculate your insurance needs within this range.

## F. RENEWABLE? YES

Disability insurance can be noncancellable, guaranteed renewable, or optionally renewable. The first option is the best and, not surprisingly, the most expensive. The insurer cannot terminate the policy and the premiums remain fixed until age 65. The less expensive guaranteed-renewable policy cannot be cancelled either but premiums can be raised. Optionally renewable policies are the cheapest but should be avoided: The insurer can terminate whole groups of such policies.

## REAL-LIFE DIALOGUE

QUESTION: "I own a small business. Are there any special disability policies for me?"

ANSWER: "Yes. Self-employed individuals can buy policies that include overhead-expense coverage (covers the costs of keeping the office running) and other customized benefits."

## Ready to Shop

Disability insurance, which straddles life and health insurance, is offered by carriers in both those lines of businesses. For shopping advice, consult those sections of this chapter.

## Home Insurance: Peace of Mind

Home is where the heart is. It's also where the art is, the china, and the VCR. That, plus the fact that the home represents the largest single investment of many Americans, makes homeowner's insurance—or renter's insurance—an absolute must.

Here's a quick guide to this critical subject—what it protects and what it protects against. Most importantly, this section will help you find the best buys in a field characterized by wide price variations. A Washington, D.C., survey of insurers found that premiums for the identical policy varied by more than $300 a year. Charity may begin at home, but it shouldn't begin with your insurance company.

## 1. What It Protects: Your Castle and Its Contents

Home insurance protects many things:

- Your house—or "dwelling," as insurers call it.
- Your personal property.
- Your legal liability—if Mr. Jones trips over young Gabriel's skateboard, or a house guest is bumped down the stairs by your friendly dog.
- Hotel and restaurant bills if a fire or some other disaster makes it impossible to use your home.

And there's more. Standard homeowner's policies also cover any detached structures on your property—your garage, gazebo, etc. Trees and shrubs are covered too, within limits (in insurance, there are always limits). And if calamity finds you outside the home—say your portable computer is stolen in the city—your homeowner's policy may also protect you.

## 2. What It Protects Against: Falls, Fires, and More

Forty-nine of the fifty states follow a standard home insurance system that classifies policies by their range of coverage.

### BASIC (HO-1)

Protects your dwelling and its contents against eleven kinds of hazards, from such likely ones as fire and theft to unlikely events like volcanic eruptions.

### BROAD (HO-2)

Includes all eleven HO-1 protections, plus damage from frozen pipes, falling objects, water leaks, a flooded basement, and assorted other perils.

### SPECIAL (HO-3)

Includes all HO-1 and HO-2 protections plus all others— except those explicitly excluded in the policy. Wars and nuclear accidents are two customary exclusions.

These are the most common homeowner's policies. Of course, their premiums rise as coverage broadens from category to category. Renters have their own standard form, HO-4, which is basically analogous to HO-2 for homeowners, as do owners of condominiums (HO-6) and older homes (HO-8).

Which level of coverage is right for you depends on your situation, your budget, and how much risk you feel comfortable living with. If water damage is a real worry for you, you may want to choose Broad over Basic coverage since the latter does not shield against such a mishap. And if you want protection against floods, or earthquakes (a good idea if you're shaking and baking in sunny California), you'll need a special policy. No standard home policies offer such protection, not even the HO-3 version.

(Note to Texans: Yep, your state is the only one to have different, though very similar, homeowner insurance categories.)

## 3. Moat and All:
## What's Your Castle Worth?

Now that you're all jittery from this list of possible calamities—do I smell smoke?—let's figure out how much insurance is right for you. Renters can skip this section.

Simple, you say. Your house cost $200,000, so you'll need that much insurance. Wrong! The price you paid for your house is a dangerous yardstick for insurance. If you bought when the market was low, your purchase price is now too small to give you adequate coverage. Even your dwelling's current market value is no good since market prices include the land, which doesn't need insurance. Your mortgage is also an unsuitable standard.

The right measure of insurance on your house is its replacement value—the cost of rebuilding should disaster strike. To find that figure you'll need an appraiser, who will consider the size of your house, the average square-foot construction costs in your town, and other factors.

High construction costs mean high replacement costs—and that means high premiums for you. But there is some good news: Your policy doesn't need to cover 100% of your home's replacement cost because homes are seldom totally destroyed. You should insure at least 80% of your home—both to protect you fully against dev-

astating events and to avoid the less favorable payment
rules insurers apply to less coverage. NOTE: Your mortgage company may insist on full replacement coverage,
mine does.

---

### REAL-LIFE TIP

Appraiser's fees can be chunky. But banks and insurers
sometimes offer free appraisal services.

---

## 4. Your Stuff: Make a List, Check It Twice

Stuff. We all have more of it than we think: cameras,
Cuisinarts, candlesticks. The most important part of this
aspect of home insurance is to take inventory. Go from
room to room and drawer to drawer making a list of all
your possessions—clothes, appliances, furniture. Gather
receipts, dates of purchase, and serial and model numbers. Take photos or a videotape of each large item, and
do the same with each wall in the house.

Next, take your records and copy them. Keep one set
at home—in a fireproof strongbox perhaps—and keep
the other set in a secure place outside the home, such as
your safe deposit box. This elaborate exercise accom-
plishes two things:

- It lets you know what you have.
- It provides you with a complete record of your possessions, which will make it much easier to get
  reimbursed by your insurer.

## 5. What! Only $50 For My Technics CD Player?

What's all your stuff worth, sentimental value aside? Homeowner policies have a standard three-part answer.

- Your personal property is insured for up to 50% of your home's coverage. So a $150,000 policy on your house means that you get an extra $75,000 of protection for your stuff.
- But, remember, there are strict limits on paybacks for valuable items like furs or jewelry. The typical limits are $1,000 to $3,000. Yes, even for Grandma's Tiffany wedding ring!
- Your benefits are computed on a cash value basis, which is an "as is" measure that applies discounts for defects and wear and tear. For example, if the knob has to be jiggled in order for your TV to work, it is defective and worth that much less.

### RENTERS: GET REAL!

While 96% of homeowners have home insurance, only 41% of renters do. This is dangerous because the landlord's insurance typically covers only the building structure itself, leaving the renter's personal property uninsured.

If you don't like these standard terms you can vary them, but it will boost your premium. For instance, for those with lots of valuables (or very modest houses), insurers may be willing to cover your personal property for up to 75% of the house coverage.

For particularly valuable items, policyholders can purchase a *personal articles floater*, which provides additional protection for itemized belongings.

Finally, policyholders can request replacement-value coverage for their personal property. Replacement-value coverage doesn't discount your goods for wear and tear. This request will boost your premium by 10% to 15%, but some might prefer it.

## 6. Liability:
## The Icy Sidewalk and Other Mishaps

Homeowner's insurance protects more than a dwelling and its contents. It also shields the policyholder from personal liability for injuries sustained by others at the home and for damage and injuries caused outside the home by the insured or members of his family. In REAL terms, this means you're protected when Ms. Bell slips on your icy sidewalk, or your darling Laura lofts a rock through her picture window.

Standard homeowner's policies offer $100,000 to $300,000 of liability insurance, which also covers lawyer's fees and other expenses in addition to paying a court judgment or agreed-upon settlement. Unlike the dwelling-and-contents portion of the policy, where deductibles of $250 and up apply, there is no deductible for liability insurance.

RAINY DAY NOTE

Standard liability coverage may be sufficient for many. But for others, high jury awards in personal-injury lawsuits may make an umbrella policy—extra liability coverage—a very prudent move for that "rainy day" when one of your trees may fall on a passing car causing the driver to black out and run into your neighbor's newly remodeled home. Since these policies only go into effect after the basic policy—called the underlying coverage—has been exhausted, they are not too expensive.

Umbrellas are usually sold by insurers who offer home and auto policies, to which umbrellas are customarily linked. Also, umbrellas can cover additional types of lawsuits—libel, invasion of privacy, etc.—that are excluded from the homeowner's policy liability coverage.

## 7. Home (Insurance) Shopping Network

We're almost home, so to speak. You know how much insurance you want and your inventory of personal property is locked away in your safe deposit box. But how do you locate the insurer with the best buy? Simple. Just follow these steps:

- CALL several insurance agents or brokers for premium quotes. Also, your state insurance department may have comparative-price data.
- ASK friends, relatives, and your state insurance department about the service and claims records of the companies that interest you. Nothing replaces service when mishaps occur—the whole point of insurance is for someone to be there, on your side and at your side, when the going gets tough.
- TAKE the highest deductible you can reasonably tol-

erate, and use your savings to buy additional insurance if you need it. By bumping your deductible from $250 to $500, for instance, you can save enough to get more liability coverage.

- INSTALL fire and burglar alarms. These can lower your premiums. You may also get a break if you live within a certain distance from a fire hydrant.
- READ your policy backwards. The last pages are where the exclusions are usually buried—the things the insurer will not cover with this policy.

---

**REAL-LIFE TIP**

Review your coverage regularly. That new bathroom in the cellar, or bay window in the dining room, may raise your insurance needs.

---

# Auto Insurance:
# Drive Hard For Values

The big lesson in auto insurance is to put a brake on premiums. New York State recently found that insurers were charging between $362 and $655 for the same exact coverage. So, comparison shopping is worthwhile—especially when today's average rates are so expensive.

This section is a roadmap to bargains. After learning the basics of the business, you'll learn what coverage you don't need (like collision insurance on a bucket of bolts), what discounts you can get (with airbags, for instance) and how to seek premium quotes from reputable insurers.

(Some REAL advice to those tempted to forego auto insurance. That's illegal, and it's also a big mistake. True, insurance costs a lot, but consider this: There were 34.4 million car accidents in 1989, leading to 47,000 deaths, 5.5 million injuries, and $94 billion in economic losses. Enough said? Oh, there were 1.5 million car thefts that year too.)

## 1. The Nuts and Bolts
Its sold as a package, but car insurance protects you from six different dangers, and each protection has its own price tag:

### A. LIABILITY FOR INJURY OR DEATH
Covers pedestrians, passengers in your car, and passengers in other cars.

### B. LIABILITY FOR PROPERTY DAMAGE
You skid and squash your neighbor's prize roses.

### C. COLLISION DAMAGE
Dents and worse to your car.

### D. COMPREHENSIVE CAR DAMAGE
Other perils to your car besides collision—theft or fire, for example.

E. MEDICAL COSTS
Doctor bills, etc., for you, your passengers, and others.


F. UNINSURED MOTORIST MISHAPS
Medical bills for you or your family when the person legally liable is an uninsured or underinsured driver.

---

### REAL-LIFE TIP

Worried about wrecking a rental? Don't be. Most people are covered under their own auto policy, even when driving a rented vehicle. So, when rental agents pressure you to pay for a collision damage waiver (CDW), politely decline. It's a big profit center for car rental companies but it's unnecessary protection that'll cost you $7 to $13 a day. Usually, the same rules apply for liability insurance although rental companies generally don't give you the "hard sell" on this type of coverage.

---

Generally, car insurance covers you and anyone else who drives your car with your permission. It also covers you or any of your licensed family members when driving someone else's car.

Most states require some car insurance, such as medical payments (E above) and liability coverage (A and B). But the types and amounts required vary, and liability coverage minimums are always too low. For example, New York State's $10,000 minimum for bodily injury liability insurance wouldn't make a dent, so to speak, in the seven-digit jury awards reported daily in the newspaper.

*No-fault note*: Fifteen states and Puerto Rico are no-fault jurisdictions, where insurers pay their own policyholders' claims regardless of who caused the accident. In "fault" states, accidents often spark long and costly lawsuits over which driver is at fault, because that fact affects which insurer pays. No-fault states also restrict lawsuits to very severe accidents. In essence, no-fault is a trade-off. Motorists get paid faster on claims, but they usually lose the right to sue. *Bottom Line*: The basics of insurance shopping are the same in fault and no-fault states.

---

### REAL-LIFE TIP

Take a car pool to work? Let your agent know: The less you drive the lower your premiums.

---

## 2. Custom Build Your Policy

Car insurance is a package of parts, much like a car. Depending on your situation, some parts may be options and some may be necessary equipment. Here's a checklist to help you steer toward your best choices:

### A. LIABILITY INSURANCE: GO DELUXE

Lawsuits can ruin you, and lawyer's fees can ruin you even if you win. This means that you should have enough liability insurance to cover your assets—even though liability protection can grow to be 40% or 50% of your total car premium. Experts recommend $300,000 per accident, and folks with sizable estates may also want an "umbrella" policy that provides $1 million or more in extra coverage.

B. COLLISION AND COMPREHENSIVE

No frills. Together, these two components protect your car from accident, theft, vandalism, and other perils—except mechanical problems. They comprise 30% to 40% of the total car insurance bill. The big question is whether your car is worth it. If it's a new luxury roadster, yes. But if it's a rust bucket, the answer is no because insurers never pay more than the car's book value. BEST ADVICE: Take as high a deductible on "*C* and *C*" as you comfortably can. The money you save on premiums can buy more liability protection.

C. DUPLICATE COVERAGE: STEER CLEAR!

If you have an "umbrella" liability policy on your house or apartment, remember that it typically applies to your car insurance too. And if your health insurance policy is good, you may not need auto medical-payment coverage unless lots of nonrelatives drive or ride in your vehicle.

---

## REAL-LIFE WORRY

QUESTION: "I had a bad accident but it wasn't my fault. Are my rates going to go through the roof?"

ANSWER: "Probably not. But if you're at fault, had a number of recent accidents (your fault or not), or received a ticket for drunk driving or some other serious offense, your rates will likely go up when your current policy expires. And keep in mind that, like all other prices, premiums rise with inflation—whatever your driving record may be."

## 3. Follow The Road To Low Rates

Many factors affect car insurance rates. If you're a male under twenty-five years, for instance, you're more likely to be a hot-rodder and you'll be required to pay higher rates. Some other rate determinants include the area in which you live, your driving record, and any driver education you may have had. Some factors, like your age, sex, and marital status, can't easily be changed, but others can:

### A. CAR MODEL
Some cars cost more to insure because they are more likely to be stolen, more likely to be driven faster, less able to withstand crashes, or more expensive to fix (#1 stolen small sedan in 1989: Volkswagen Jetta). Consult your local library for information sources on this subject.

### B. PROTECTIVE DEVICES
You can get rate reductions of 5% to 30% if your car has antitheft mechanisms or safety devices such as airbags, automatic seat belts, or antilock brakes.

### C. MULTIPOLICY DEALS
Many insurers sell homeowner's, auto, and umbrella insurance, and offer discounts to customers who buy more than one policy.

### D. HEALTHY HABITS
It's no surprise that nondrinking drivers get a discount but nonsmokers sometimes do too. The reason: Watch

someone fumble for a cigarette on the interstate. They should also give discounts to people who don't use audiocassettes, brush their teeth (yes, I've seen this), shave, or put on makeup while driving.

## REAL-TOUGH PROBLEM

QUESTION: "I'm a young male driver with a so-so driving record. I've checked with several insurers and no one will touch me. What can I do?"

ANSWER: "Ask your state insurance department for the names of insurers in your state who specialize in high-risk drivers. If you still have trouble, ask the department about the state's assigned risk plan. You can't be turned down by this plan but the insurance will be expensive."

## 4. Forget the Car: Let Your Fingers Do the Walking!

Don't run out of gas yet, you're almost home! You know which of the six types of car insurance you want, how much coverage you need, and some ways to lower your premiums. But the best way to put a "dent" in car rates is to shop around. Check with your friends and consult consumer guides to generate a list of good companies among the nation's 3,500 car insurers.

Ask at least a half-dozen insurers for premium quotes for the specific coverage you've chosen. Get quotes for different deductibles too to see how they affect the total cost.

But remember to keep your eyes on the road. Price is not the only issue. Ask your state's insurance department and your other sources about the claims records and general service reputation of several of your lowest-price insurers. Your state may also compile complaint records for each company. Narrow your search to include only the top-rated companies.

CASE IN POINT: In mid-1991, New York accused thirteen auto insurers of failing to provide promised premium rebates to those policyholders who installed safety and antitheft devices in their vehicles. While admitting no wrongdoing (do they ever?), the insurers had to pay $5 million to a pool of 200,000 New Yorkers.

---

## Health Insurance: No Cure in Sight

---

It's enough to make you sick! Our health care industry is ailing, and we're all going to catch it. Even if you're young and healthy, even if you're single with no dependents, and even if you're covered at work, you're not immune to the growing ills of the American health care system.

Consider this: In 1965, the average American spent $176 on health care. By 1988, this figure had soared to $2,124. In 1965, private health insurers paid $5.7 billion in claims. In 1988, the number rose to $171 billion. Given these galloping costs, insurers are offering less coverage for more money and imposing new requirements on policyholders—like getting permission before you go to the hospital.

Caught in the middle, employers are pulling back too. In 1989, 56% of employers paid 100% of health insurance premiums. Just two years later, this figure had dropped to 48%.

Everyone needs health insurance. But these gloomy trends make it even more necessary to make sure you have adequate coverage. Here's a how-to:

## 1. The Basics
## (Take Two Aspirin Before Reading)

Health insurance is the most complex of all insurance. There are no standard forms, and the variations are endless. But there are two primary parts to it:

### A. BASIC PROTECTION

Covers the costs of short-term illnesses and injuries, including doctor visits, surgery, and hospital stays.

### B. MAJOR MEDICAL

Applies to catastrophic, long-term health problems, often picking up the hospital, medical, and surgical bills where basic coverage leaves off. If your health-insurance dollars are limited, this is the coverage you should get. It shields you from financial ruin.

There are other kinds of policies and they are sometimes valuable. But they are supplements to these two primary types of coverage.

The supplemental options include "hospital indemnity" policies, which pay a cash benefit, say $50, for each hospital day beyond a certain minimum. Another type is the "dread disease" policy, which pertains only to a particular, and particularly feared ailment—cancer, AIDS, or heart disease, for example. Experts say to stay away from these policies because you are better off simply buying more general health insurance with those dollars.

A third supplemental policy is disability insurance. Covered elsewhere in this chapter, these policies do not pay for your health care but do cover your income lost because of a sickness or accident.

## 2. Policies:
### Individual, Group, and More

Most Americans are covered by group health plans at work. These are the best buys by far, often having low premiums, good coverage, full or partial employer payment of premiums, and no required medical exams. Group coverage is also available from some professional associations, alumni clubs, and fraternal organizations. These group offerings, however, are not always as attractive as the workplace variety.

Individual policies are expensive. But they are the only private-insurance options for the self-employed, the unemployed, and those in jobs without insurance.

For those over 65 there is Medicare. But since Medicare covers only about 40% of a person's health costs, seven out of ten seniors supplement it with a "wraparound" policy or "Medigap." These policies are specifically designed to plug the holes in Medicare coverage.

For the eligible poor there is Medicaid. For the growing number of ineligible poor, there is the bleak world of uninsurance. Amazingly, more than 26 million Americans *with jobs* have no health insurance. It has simply gotten too expensive even for many of those in the so-called "middle class."

## SHOPPER'S TIP

Many employees can now choose between conventional insurance and a health maintenance organization (HMO). When comparing your options, remember that HMOs often cover preventive care, but sharply limit your choice of doctors. And while HMO participants avoid the bothersome claims paperwork of regular insurance, some experts contend that the fixed budgets of HMOs may encourage them to cut corners on medical care. There's also an alphabet soup of HMO offshoots including independent practice organizations (IPOs) and preferred provider organizations (PPOs). These arrangements have somewhat fewer restrictions on your choice of doctors than HMOs.

## 3. Diagnosing Your Policy

Easy so far? Wait, your migraine headache is still in its infancy. If you are in the market for an individual policy, you must understand the complexities of the field. If you are covered at work, you still need to determine if you need supplemental coverage because we live in an age of health-cost cutbacks. Here's the most palatable medicine we found for both of these groups.

THE TOP 7 COUNTDOWN OF HEALTH INSURANCE

1. COBRA: LEARN ITS RULES. When death, divorce, or an unplanned departure from a job occurs, a worker and his or her dependents may have their health coverage affected. Such situations are governed by a 1985 federal law, the Consolidated Omnibus Budget Reconciliation Act (COBRA), which guarantees continued group coverage for up to 18 months if you are fired or laid off from a job and 36 months for the spouse or other dependents of an insured worker who is "terminated." The former employee can be charged 100% of what the employer had been paying, plus a processing charge.

2. DEDUCTIBLES: DEFEND AGAINST DISASTER. Get as high a deductible as you can manage and use your premium savings to increase your coverage to $1 million or more. Rationale: The aim of insurance is to shield you in the case of a disaster. If you must foot a high deductible for such protection, don't hesitate to do so.

3. PREEXISTING CONDITIONS: WATCH CLOSELY. Insurers often exclude benefits for medical conditions that began before the policy did. *Remedy*: Seek preexisting condition clauses that cover only already-diagnosed problems, not latent ones that you didn't know about. Also: All such clauses will eventually cover those conditions but make

sure that the waiting period—sometimes as long as two years—is not too long for you.

4. KNOW YOUR COSTS. Premiums are only one cost. Others are the deductible and coinsurance, which obligates policyholders to pay, say, the first $200 of each year's expenses and 20% of additional bills. Coinsurance often has a stop-loss provision, which places a yearly cap on the amount you are required to pay. *Advice*: Buy a policy with a stop-loss provision.

5. INSIDE LIMITS: UPDATE THEM. Some policies offer specific dollar benefits for claims. This can be chancy. For example, if your policy offers $200 per hospital day and you know that $500 is the norm, you would be liable for the $300 difference. *Remedies*: You can buy a hospital-indemnity policy to raise your per diem hospital coverage but it's better to get a policy with "service benefits." Unlike "inside limits," service benefits do not specify a dollar figure, and are less likely to become outdated by health-cost inflation. *Caution*: Service benefits are often based on fees deemed to be "reasonable" in your area. This means that you may not be fully covered if you use a high-priced physician.

6. MAJOR MEDICAL: RAISE YOUR CAP. Major medical policies often have lifetime caps of $100,000, $250,000, or $500,000. In an era of $500-a-day hospital beds, these caps may turn out to be too low. *Remedy*: Raise the limit to $1 million or more. Watch out! Some policies have annual caps, too.

7. EXCLUSIONS: CHECK THEM OUT. Health care policies often have laundry lists of excluded conditions and services. Read them closely. Common exclusions are chiropractic and psychiatric care, prescription drugs, diagnostic procedures, private duty nurses, and preventive medicine (checkups, etc.). *Beware*: Some "inclusions" are less equal than others. Psychiatric expenses, for example, may be covered, but only at 50%.

*Note*: COBRA applies only to workers at companies with twenty or more employees, but some states have added supplemental statutes. If COBRA does not apply to you, ask your former employer if you can convert your group policy to an individual one.

---

### SHOPPER'S TIP

Have kids? Check the policy to see at what age their coverage ends and whether they can convert to a policy of their own without a medical exam.

---

## 4. Compare and Contrast

Choosing a health insurer is as crucial as choosing a doctor. Select an insurer who is licensed in your state and ask your state insurance department for information about rates and reputations of insurers. Check A.M. Best and other sources—available at your library—for information on each insurer's financial strength. And:

A. LOOK AT LOSS RATIOS

This measures the portion of the premiums that are paid out in benefits to policyholders. The higher the better. Not-for-profit Blue Cross/Blue Shield often exceeds 90% loss ratios. Good numbers for commercial insurers are 80% to 90% for group coverage, and 60% or more for individual policies.

B. TAKE THE TEN-DAY TRIAL

If you buy a health policy, you are entitled to a ten-day "free look," and a full refund if you don't like what you see.

C. STUDY THE DEDUCTIBLE

Make sure your deductible applies to each year and not to each illness. Yes, they may try to slip this in!

---

## REAL-LIFE TIP

Tired of health-claims paperwork? Having trouble getting correct insurance reimbursement? A new industry has grown up to handle these problems, taking on these chores for a relatively modest fee. With names like Claims Recovery and Health Claims Assistance, these companies may also be useful to those procrastinators who may have thousands of dollars owed to them because they've never taken the time to file claims. To find help in your area, call the National Association of Claims Assistance Professionals (NACAP) at 708-963-3500. And, as always, check out prospective companies with your state and local consumer protection agencies.

# Planning Ahead

We've already talked about the need for certain types of insurance and the importance of starting your investment regimen early. In the next chapter we will discuss the difficult task of caring for an elderly or disabled relative. What's left then? In preparing for the future, there are some other things that you'll need to consider. This chapter considers some of these things and the importance of thinking ahead when it comes to specific matters like your health, legal matters, and "final arrangements."

One subject we will not cover in this chapter is estate planning. Estate planning is an extremely complicated area that we have already covered in some detail in the preceding section on insurance and an upcoming chapter on investing.

# Wills

It may be true that the chances of dying suddenly are quite small. But why is it that just one third of Americans have a will when they do die? How can it be that so many people, at least some of whom must be at least familiar with the subject of wills, fail to have one made?

It could be our collective inability to deal with the issue of death. Or maybe it's just plain laziness. In any case, a great deal of chaos, and very profitable legal work, is created by persons who die without wills. Whether it's for an elderly relative or yourself, writing a will makes good common sense.

## 1. What is a Will?
In plain vanilla terms, a will is a legal document that expresses our wishes for the guardianship of children, and the distribution of property, at the time we die.

## 2. Why Do We Need a Will?
A will helps to assure that our wishes are respected when we leave the material world. Without a will, relatives, friends, or even acquaintances and business associates, can fight for custody of children, argue over the rights to property, or fail to abide by your heartfelt desire to be stuffed and placed alongside your dog, Fido, in the living room.

## 3. "But I'm Single and Don't Have Any Children"
In the event of your death, inheritance laws will give all of your property to your parents. Do you want your parents to have your prize collection of Elvis Presley memorabilia? A will enables you to decide what things are given to particular people or institutions. Without a will, you voluntarily give up the right to make your own decisions regarding the disposition of your assets. You'll also increase the likelihood that your family and friends will fight for the right to keep your stuff.

*Real Conclusion:* There is absolutely no point in your adult life when a will should be considered optional.

## REAL NIGHTMARE: DYING WITHOUT A WILL

(Read in Rod Serling voice) Imagine, if you will, the following scenario: In your avoidance of certain REAL-life issues, you failed to see a lawyer about a will. As a result, following you and your spouse's untimely death in an amusement park accident, your kids, and the bulk of your hard-earned money, are given to your sister-in-law and her abusive gambling-addicted husband.

And what may be worse, your beloved Labrador retrievers are given over to the local dog pound. If this scenario doesn't get you to make a will, nothing can.

We often hear gruesome stories about family disputes over children and assets of a deceased relative. Disgusting, but just another one of life's REAL problems. And while a will may not keep your relatives out of court, it will make it more difficult for anyone to contest your wishes.

## 4. Who Can Prepare a Will?

It probably makes sense to use a competent lawyer. Low-cost, write-your-own will kits simply cannot address the complex and ever-changing nature of today's tax laws. Your lawyer can discuss your specific situation with you and create a document that should withstand any contest.

## 5. How Much Will It Cost?

A relatively simple will should cost no more than $300 to $400. Married persons usually make their own individual wills. If you have complicated trusts, or are involved in partnerships or other business relationships, the costs of creating a will may be higher.

## 6. What Do You Need to Consider?

Depending on your situation, you'll need to consider the following questions when writing your will:

### A. WHO WILL GET YOUR ASSETS?

Think about your spouse, children, grandchildren, other relatives, charities, etc.

### B. WHO WILL BE NAMED GUARDIAN?

In other words, who will be given custody of your children, if you have any who have not yet reached legal age? Think about this question carefully. This is probably your most important decision.

*Important:* Don't put off making a will because your wife wants her mother to take the kids if you both die, and you simply won't hear of this. You can find a compromise.

Paul Levis, a financial planner in New York, suggests that clients in this situation make the following arrangement. If they should die in an odd-numbered year, the wife has her wishes respected and the children go to her mother. If, on the other hand, they die in an even-numbered year, the husband has his wishes followed. Sort of like a morbid Russian roulette. Remember, a will can always be revised if your feelings change.

## C. WHERE AND HOW YOU WANT TO BE BURIED

Personally, I want to be cremated and have my ashes sprinkled from a helicopter over the National Tennis Center. You may want to be buried at sea. Others may want to be cremated and placed in a favorite jar. If you have any special requests, they should be clearly stated in your will.

## D. WHO WILL BE NAMED EXECUTOR?

Contrary to what this name may suggest, an executor does not eliminate those enemies you made during your natural life. Instead, an executor ensures that your will's instructions are actually carried out. In the case of a married couple, each person usually names their spouse. In the unlikely event that both persons die, an outside person should be named to fill this role.

Your executor should always know where to find your will. They'll need to provide the original document, not a copy, to the court. Remember, being an executor can be a lot of work, so be sure to ask a friend or relative for permission before naming him or her.

In some states, executors are entitled to commissions based on a fixed percentage of the estate's assets. This fee can be waived and, while a friend or relative will not usually ask for compensation, choosing a lawyer for this role can run into substantial costs. In general, your executor should work with your attorney to fulfill his or her duties.

*Safe Deposit Boxes:* In many states, your safe deposit box is sealed at the time of your death by your friends at the

IRS. Because of this, most experts advise against keeping your original will in a safe deposit box. Most people keep their will with their lawyer.

If you want a friend or relative to have access to your safe deposit box, make certain that they have a key—and permission to gain access. Instruct this person to get to the bank as soon after your death as possible and clear out all items. Any important documents should be secured before the bank seals the box for inspection by the IRS.

### E. WHO WILL BE NAMED TRUSTEE?

If needed, this person will manage any assets that are put into trust (not given directly to a beneficiary). Make certain that this person shares your investment philosophy and won't run off to Pago Pago with your children's college fund. Remember, best friends don't always make the best trustees.

## 7. How Often Do I Need to Update My Will?

Generally speaking, you should review your will every five years. However, you will need to revise your will if any of the following events occur:

- You move to a different state.
- The laws of your state change significantly.
- Your assets change considerably.
- You get married or divorced.
- A child or grandchild is born or adopted.

- Your children reach legal age.
- Any beneficiary dies.

---

## REAL PAIN: PROBATE

Probate is the process during which a judge determines the validity of your will. Your executor, usually working with your attorney, must present your will to a probate court. The court then decides if the will is legally binding.

---

## 8. Why Do People Hate Probate?

Probate can be time-consuming and expensive. Depending on the complexity of your will, and whether or not it is contested, the administrative process can take several years to complete and cost as much as 20% of your estate's value. Generally speaking, the simpler the will the less costly, and time-consuming, the probate process.

*Good News:* The probate process is being simplified in many states.

## 9. What If I Die Without a Valid Will?

This is called dying intestate. In this case, the court writes your will for you, according to the laws and provisions of your state. This includes the distribution of your wealth, guardianship of your children, etc. Pretty scary, huh? Solution: Get a Will!

**REAL ADVICE**

Be sure to include an inventory for your heirs and executors. Details should include:
• Your social security number.
• Bank account names, locations, and numbers.
• Insurance company policies.
• Stock and mutual fund accounts.
• Credit card accounts.
• Location and details of other property.
• Names and addresses of lawyers, accountants, brokers, doctors, etc.

# Living Wills

Living wills have grown in usage over the past few years. More than one in five Americans now have one, and that number is growing rapidly. Simply put, a living will is a legal document that expresses your medical desires at the time you may become comatose or otherwise unable to express your own wishes.

As the population ages, and more Americans are hospitalized, the need for living wills is becoming more widely recognized. According to a recent Gallup poll, more than three-quarters of all Americans say they would like to have a living will at some point in the future.

Federal law now requires that hospitals, nursing homes, hospices, home-health agencies, and health-maintenance organizations inform patients in writing of their rights to preplan their life and death decisions.

## What Does a Living Will Say?

A living will states your wishes concerning the extent of medical treatment you want to receive in the event you are incapacitated and cannot communicate for yourself. Most commonly, this involves the use of life-support systems when there is little hope for recovery.

### REAL PRECAUTION:

Even though a majority of states now respect these documents, living wills can be contested. In most of these cases, a family member fights to keep a loved one alive at any cost. To further protect your rights, make sure your living will is very specific. You should also execute an appropriate document giving some trusted person a health-care power of attorney. This person becomes your advocate and is allowed to make your health care decisions when you cannot.

They can help in the event that family members, or even local religious groups, don't agree with your instructions.

It's important to note that 80% of Americans die in hospitals. Of those, 70% have to make decisions regarding life-support.

## Living Wills: Important to Remember:

1. Use an attorney, or get free copies of the proper forms for your state from the Society for the Right to Die/Concern for Dying (200 Varick Street, New York, NY 10014).
2. Discuss your provisions with your doctor and make certain that he or she will respect your wishes. If not, find one who will.
3. Name only one person to hold your health care power of attorney. Avoid naming "my family" or any other group of persons who may disagree among themselves. You may want to name an alternate in case your first choice is unavailable when the critical time comes.
4. Review your living will, and your health care power of attorney, every two to three years.
5. Express your wishes to family members. This way, they may be less likely to act against your instructions.
6. Complete multiple forms if you maintain residences in more than one state.

# 5 $ 🏠 🚗 🎓 ❤️

# Caring for an Elderly Relative

## "How Am I *Ever* Going to Deal With This?"

Let's face it: Life is hard. As one popular bumper sticker warns us, "Life's a Bitch Then You Die." Things may not have gotten that bad, but most of us do have it tough, with children, demanding jobs, working spouses, and assorted other stresses on our limited time and financial resources. Making matters even more difficult for some of us is the aging of our parents. Like us, they're getting older. But in the case of our parents, they'll be needing an increasing amount of our help, adding to those many existing burdens on our precious time and energy.

It's called the "graying of America." There are now 30 million seniors in the country, making up about 12% of the population. By the year 2000—less than a decade away—the total will be 40 to 45 million, or a full 20% of the country. And the country will only get grayer as we move through the next millenium.

This single demographic change will put unprecedented pressures on our society. For one thing, the nation's health care costs will soar. It's predicted that by the year 2000, seniors will account for one half of the country's total health costs, up from less than one third today. The country's nursing homes, already housing 2.3 million Americans, will be home to 5.3 million Americans by the year 2000.

And who will be among those facing this burden? Why, us of course. It's estimated that more than 2.7 million adult children are already caring for aging parents and 37% of today's women can expect to do so at some point in their lives. Many of us will actually spend more time caring for aging parents than raising our own kids.

Making matters worse: More than half of today's seniors haven't made any plans for their housing needs in their later years. Fortunately, there are a growing number of options to choose from, including new kinds of senior residences, from accessory apartments to "ECHO" housing and lifecare communities, that create meaningful alternatives to nursing homes. Meanwhile, new financing techniques, like long-term care insurance and reverse mortgages, can help many to meet the prohibitive costs of growing old in America. And, through the work of support groups and such new options as "respite care," there is a growing recognition of the demands and stresses on caregivers.

This section will help you deal with this growing number of choices, giving special attention to in-home care and strategies for protecting your family's assets from nursing home and other health care bills. Most importantly, this chapter will give you a step-by-step plan to deal with this complicated and emotionally charged stage of REAL life.

# But First: A Word About You

We are being called the "sandwich" generation caught between the demands of young and old loved ones (not to mention jobs, spouses, educational goals, financial concerns, etc.). In these times, caring for an elderly relative can prove to be especially stressful and exhausting.

Nothing in this book, or anywhere for that matter, is going to magically erase these burdens for you. But there are ways to lighten your load. First, remember you're not alone. The graying of America has sparked the growth of hundreds of public and private groups dedicated to helping seniors and their caregivers. Many of these helpers are described throughout this chapter.

The five groups listed below offer excellent eldercare assistance. Consult them for information and assistance on important eldercare issues, from shopping for nursing homes to managing caregiver stress to finding the best cushion-lift chairs and other senior products. There may be other agencies operating within your state, county, or municipality that can also offer important assistance.

### 1. AREA AGENCIES ON AGING (AAA)
There are 600 federally mandated AAA offices throughout the country. They provide information and referrals on housing, Medicare, taxes, and other issues. To contact

the AAA office nearest you, call the National Association
of Area Agencies on Aging at 800-677-1116.

2. AMERICAN ASSOCIATION OF RETIRED PERSONS (AARP)
The largest and most powerful senior-citizen group in the
country, AARP was founded in 1958. AARP provides free
literature and advice on most eldercare issues. Call them
at 202-872-4700.

3. AMERICAN ASSOCIATION OF HOMES FOR THE AGING
(AAHA)
An association of not-for-profit nursing homes and other
eldercare residences, AAHA offers extensive materials
regarding senior housing options. Call them at 202-
783-2242.

4. NATIONAL CONSUMERS LEAGUE (NCL)
The pioneer in its field, NCL furnishes caregivers with
tough-minded, "consumerist" literature on the selection
and use of services for seniors, including home health-
care, hospice care, and long-term care. Call them at
202-639-8140.

5. CHILDREN OF AGING PARENTS (CAPS)
CAPS is a national clearinghouse on eldercare. Among
other things, it focuses on the psychological and emotional aspects of aging and caregiver stress, and helps to
start caregiver support groups throughout the country.
You're not alone! Call them at 215-945-6900.

    Also, try to join a support group in your area.

Meetings are often listed in local newspapers. You can also call your local hospital or health-care facility for information. Speaking with others in your same situation, and sharing your experiences, can be reassuring. These meetings can also be an excellent source of information regarding the legal, medical, psychological, and social aspects of caring for an elderly relative.

# Planning Ahead I: "Where Are All the Papers?"

Old age and its ailments often bring a decline in a person's ability to manage his or her financial and legal affairs. Warning signs of the decline include disorganized paperwork, piles of unopened mail, communications from collection agencies, etc. An aging relative's affairs can become an expensive and uncorrectable mess if things are allowed to go too far. So, as is true with so many things, early planning is the key to success. Take these steps while your loved one is still healthy and competent. It may be uncomfortable talking to an able person about his possible decline, but the alternatives can be much worse.

## 1. GO THROUGH THE PAPERS
Learn the financial basics: your relative's income, expenses, investments, insurance policies, will, and other financial and legal data. Make and keep a list of account

numbers, balances, and contact phone numbers, and
know where important documents—like the will and the
insurance policies—are kept. Also familiarize yourself
with your relative's network: his or her lawyer, accountant, banker, broker, etc.

### 2. TAKE STOCK

Are your relative's financial arrangements appropriate for
his or her stage in life? Perhaps the will should be updated. Are all premiums and other bills paid? Are all
checks cashed? To reduce your loved one's paperwork,
consider direct deposit of checks and automatic payment
of bills (more companies are offering this service). Investments may need to be reordered, from growth-oriented ones to safer, income-producing, types.

### 3. ASSIST IN MONEY MANAGEMENT

Sooner or later, your relative may need help in managing
his or her affairs. If nothing is done until incompetence
sets in, a guardian must be appointed by a court to manage matters—an expensive and sometimes lengthy legal
process. To avoid guardianship, explore the following
ways to authorize you or another to handle things:

A. POWER OF ATTORNEY. Your relative—the "principal"—can
designate you "the attorney in fact" to pay bills, make investments, handle real estate transactions, and so on.

There are many different kinds of power of attorney.
Some apply only to a real estate closing or other specific
transaction, and expire immediately after that event oc-

curs. For caregivers of aging relatives, the best power of attorney is broad—covering all financial affairs—and "durable"—continuing in force after your relative becomes incompetent. Durable powers of attorney can also be "springing"—meaning they only take effect if and when incompetence sets in.

Powers of attorney can be revoked at any time, and you have a strict legal duty to act in your relative's best interests. A lawyer can draw up "powers" for you, but for most people the standard forms available in many libraries are sufficient. NOTE: Some banks and other institutions require that their own special "P of A" forms be used.

B. JOINT ACCOUNTS. Legally, any holder of a joint account can write checks against that account. It's an easy way for a caregiver to handle a relative's money matters without going to the trouble of a full power of attorney.

C. DEED OF ASSETS IN RETURN FOR LIFE SUPPORT. Under this legal arrangement, an elderly person hands over his or her assets to an institution or individual who agrees to support that person for life. This practice is common in continuing care retirement communities (CCRCs), an increasingly popular type of senior housing. Check with a lawyer if you're going this route.

D. TRUST AGREEMENTS. If substantial assets are involved, your relative—the "settlor"—can direct you—the "trustee"—to invest his or her assets and handle the earnings. Trusts can be constructed in many ways and can get complicated. Consult your lawyer for details.

**REAL-LIFE TIP**

The graying of America has inspired a new legal special-
ist: the Elder Law Attorney. Specializing in Medicare,
guardianship, estate planning, and other issues, these
lawyers often work hand-in-hand with social workers and
other geriatric professionals. For a national listing of specialists, write to the National Academy of Elder Law Attorneys, 655 N. Alvernon Way, Suite 108, Tucson, AZ
85711, or ask your lawyer for a referral.

E. REPRESENTATIVE PAYEE. A senior who receives Social Security or Veterans Administration payments can designate
a person to get his check and handle the funds. Forms
for this purpose can be obtained from your local office of
those federal agencies.

# Planning Ahead II: Watch the Health Gap

Finances are only one part of eldercare. One other major
part involves the time at which a person becomes terminally ill. To prepare for this eventuality, seniors should
document their desires for or against the use of life support systems and high-tech medicine with the creation of
a "living will" and a health care proxy.

Another area of major importance is health insurance.
Health care costs are rising quickly, with no end in sight.

This means that being uninsured, or even underinsured, can be disastrous.

Medicare is the health insurance system for seniors set up by the federal government. Virtually all seniors who receive Social Security are eligible for Medicare. All they need to do is fill out an application obtainable from their local Social Security office. (Enroll early—at least several months before reaching age 65.) The bad news: Medicare pays for less and less of the elderly's medical bills. At last count, Medicare covered only 45% of this group's health bills and, in the face of spiraling budget deficits, Congress is always looking at Medicare with a cutting eye. Among the current, and more sizable, gaps in Medicare Part A (hospital insurance) and Part B (medical insurance) are:

1. Medicare will pay nearly all hospital bills for the first sixty days, but there is a $652 deductible (1992 figure) before those payments start. For hospital days 61 through 90, the Medicare recipient must pay $163 a day (1992 figure), and much more for days 91 on.

2. For doctor visits, Medicare recipients must meet a $100 deductible each year, and then pay 20% of all subsequent bills, with Medicare paying the remaining 80%.

*Worse:* Medicare has caps on what it will pay doctors. If your physician charges more than the approved amount, you pay *both* the excess and your 20 percent portion up to a preset maximum.

3. Medicare will pay for all approved costs of care in a skilled nursing facility for the first twenty days; however, the patient's care needs and the facility must meet Medicare's criteria for coverage. For days 21 to 100, it pays all but $81.50 per day (1992 figure).

*Worse*: After day 100, Medicare pays nothing for skilled nursing.

4. Medicare also pays nothing for necessities like prescription drugs, eye exams, and eyeglasses, dental care and dentures, and hearing aids.

5. Medicare pays zero for custodial care—that is, the care and assistance with the routines of daily life that so many elderly desperately need.

With all of these holes, Medicare looks more like a hockey player's mouth than a comprehensive health policy. How can the elderly fill these expensive gaps in coverage? First, you should know two things:

a. No health insurance policy will substantially cover such nonhealth (nonskilled) expenses as custodial care. For that protection, seniors must look to new offerings like long-term insurance (see the next section).

b. Not all seniors need to fill these Medicare gaps on their own. Working seniors may still be covered by group policies from their employers, with Medicare acting as a supplementary policy. *Note*: Also, the elderly poor who qualify can get Medicaid, which has far fewer gaps than

Medicare. (See Section 3 for more on Medicaid eligibility.)

But most seniors—nearly 34 million as of 1992—rely on Medicare, and to fill its growing holes they need what is known as Medigap insurance. Also called Medicare supplements, Medigap policies are designed to fill many of the gaps in Medicare except long-term care—the biggest gap of all. Nearly three-quarters of all Medicare-covered seniors have bought Medigap policies.

Seniors shopping for Medigap used to have their work cut out for them. Insurers offered hundreds of confusing Medigap plans, many of which required an advanced joint degree in economics and law to understand. Many perplexed seniors, put off guard by these deceptive tactics, bought multiple policies, many of which provided duplicate coverage. Even if they could make sense of the Medigap maze, many seniors were turned down for policies because of existing health problems.

Happily, Congress has come to the rescue. Starting in January, 1992, insurers can only sell about ten standardized types of Medigap plans, making comparisons of prices and coverage much easier. The standard plans range from a "core" policy paying only for the most common Medicare gaps (annual premium: $400–$600), to a deluxe policy that greatly expands the services covered including the costs of prescription drugs, flu shots, and hearing tests ($1,200–$1,800 a year).

The new law mandated other Medigap changes too. They include:

1. NO DUPING WITH DUPLICATES

Insurers can no longer sell Medigap plans to people who already have one. In 1991, about 25% of Medigap policyholders had redundant coverage—doing nothing except filling the coffers of many insurance companies.

2. OPEN-DOOR POLICY

The law creates an "open-enrollment" rule under which no senior can be turned down for Medigap *if he or she applies within six months of enrolling in Medicare.* The rule only applies to seniors who turn 65 in May 1991 or later. *Downside*: Medigap premiums will rise as insurers pass on the costs of this "everybody in" provision.

3. CANCELLATIONS CANCELLED

As long as seniors pay their premiums, insurers cannot cancel their policies. Cancellations were always tempting to an insurer as a policyholder became older, sicker, and more expensive to carry.

## Stop! Before You Shop for Medigap

Twenty-two million elderly Americans have Medigap coverage. But there's a small and growing alternative: health maintenance organizations (HMOs). For a fixed monthly fee, the 2.1 million seniors already enrolled in HMOs get health care that's often cheaper than Medigap. Plus, they're covered for checkups, immunizations, and other preventive care that Medigap policies often neglect.

*Drawback*: Seniors who have long-standing relationships with personal physicians—as many do—may dislike HMOs, which require that you use only their staff MDs. But this also means no worrying about whether your doctor charges more than Medicare will pay.

---

### REAL-LIFE SHOPPER'S TIP

In a flap over Medigap? Even with the new federal law, Medigap shopping is tough and time-consuming. To make it easier, first contact some not-for-profit Medigap sellers like the American Association for Retired Persons (AARP), 202-872-4700, or your state's Blue Cross/Blue Shield. At a minimum, their deals will serve as a good benchmark for your comparison-shopping.

---

# Planning Ahead III:
# Take Care of Long-Term Care

If you and your older relative have negotiated the dangerous waters of Medicare and Medigap, congratulations! But your boat can still run aground on another great peril: long-term care.

As noted above, both public and private health insurance focus on, well, health. Though there are some signs of change, this means that health insurance doesn't cover long-term custodial care—the primarily nonmedical help with daily life that the old and infirm need, whether at home, in a nursing home, or in some other setting. One dramatic statistic says it all: Only 2% of the nation's nursing home bill is funded by Medicare or Medigap.

Then who does pay for long-term care? Here's the breakdown:

## 1. Private Payments

Fifty-two percent of nursing home bills—running from $52,000 to $70,000 and more each year—are paid with private funds. Private money also pays for the bulk of other eldercare options. Private funds can be exhausted quickly with such high costs, but that day can be put off with these two techniques.

### A. REVERSE MORTGAGES

Some seniors tap into their biggest asset—their home—by securing a reverse mortgage or home equity conversion. Under this arrangement, a homeowner borrows against their fully paid mortgage, thus capitalizing on the equity in their homes while still living there. The lender recoups the loan when the homeowner dies or sells the property. See chapter 3 for more on reverse mortgages.

### B. ACCELERATED DEATH BENEFITS

Some life insurance policies allow policyholders the option to receive a portion of their death benefits while they're still alive. Of course, this reduces the payment when the insured ultimately dies.

## 2. The "Spend-Down" Scenario

Even with these dollar-stretching techniques, most private monies are soon gone. And that means going on Medicaid, the state-federal health-care program for the poor.

How poor you have to be in order to be eligible for Medicaid varies from state to state. For an elderly couple with one spouse in a nursing home, state maximum monthly incomes range from $815 to about $2,000, and maximum savings vary from about $13,000 to about $75,000. To prevent impoverishment of the at-home spouse, he or she also gets to keep the house, car, jewelry, and certain other items. Check with your attorney or your local Medicaid office for the rules that apply to your specific situation.

Understandably, most people fear that going on Medicaid means the near-bankruptcy of their mates or heirs. Consequently, a cottage industry of lawyers and accountants has sprung up, dedicated to the preservation of family assets in the face of the Medicaid rules. For a referral, ask your lawyer or accountant.

Basically, these advisers say seniors should give their assets to children or other relatives, through a trust, outright gift, or other technique. And the earlier the better.

*Caution #1*: Keep enough cash on hand to finance at least six months in a nursing home. Many facilities reject applicants with too little money. Why? Because the facilities will get roughly 20% less from Medicaid residents than private payers.

*Caution #2*: The senior who is contemplating such moves should not be hasty. Once the transfer is made, he or she will lose control of the funds.

## C. LONG-TERM CARE INSURANCE

There's now another way to preserve assets besides out-foxing Medicaid. It's called long-term care insurance or nursing home insurance. Pioneered in Alaska in a 1987 state-worker contract, long-term care insurance has taken the country by storm and is now offered by more than one hundred insurance companies.

Why the quick growth? Because the policies fill the big void left by all health insurance—Medicare, Medigap, and private insurance—in payments for protracted, primarily nonmedical care.

These policies can vary greatly in benefits, premiums, and other issues. Here are the main features:

1. COVERED CARE. These policies pay for one or more of four kinds of care: skilled nursing care, intermediate nursing care, custodial care, and home care. Home care includes visits by health professionals, delivered meals, etc.

These kinds of care are not restricted to one kind of facility. Skilled nursing care can be provided at home or in a nursing home, for example, and custodial care is given in those facilities and others too.

But different policies define these types of care differently and may provide different amounts of benefit for each.

*Shopper's Note:* Be sure your policy carries significant benefits for custodial care, which is potentially the costliest and lengthiest care a senior may need.

2. BENEFITS OFFERED. Most long-term care policies offer indemnities—fixed-dollar payments, usually from $20 to $150, for each day of care received. Others pay in time—a set number of months or years of care, or for life. And some have "elimination" or "waiting" periods, which function as deductibles. Under a typical elimination provision, a senior might not collect benefits until, say, the 21st or 61st day of care received. Of course, the better your benefits, the higher your premium.

*Shopper's Note:* Fixed-payment policies expose insureds to inflation. Look for policies with cost-of-living-adjustments—COLAs—to reduce inflation risk.

3. PREMIUMS. These policies now cost anywhere from just a few hundred dollars a year to $5,000 or more. Mostly offered to people aged 50 to 79, these policies feature level premiums—they don't rise as you get older. So the younger and healthier you are when you buy, the lower your premium (but the longer you'll pay).

*Shopper's Note:* Get a "waiver of premium" provision, which suspends premium payments during periods when benefits are being received.

4. PRIOR HOSPITAL STAYS. This is a catch to watch out for. Avoid care policies that only pay for care if the insured has been in the hospital immediately beforehand. The simple fact—and insurers know it—is that many people enter nursing homes without a prior hospital stay.

5. PREEXISTING CONDITIONS. This is another peril for unwary buyers. Like health policies, long-term care policies usually will not pay, at least for some set period of time, for care needed for conditions that preceded the effective date of the policy.

*Shopper's Note:* It's hard to avoid preexisting condition clauses. But don't buy a policy if the nonpayment period is longer than six months.

6. EXCLUSIONS. The most common exclusions in standard care policies are mental and nervous disorders; alcoholism and drug addiction; and attempted suicide.

*Shopper's Note:* Some policies cover Alzheimer's disease and some do not. If such coverage is important to you, ask your agent.

Regulators are still coming to terms with long-term care insurance, a tough task since this new product is evolving rapidly. The National Association of Insurance Commissioners (NAIC) has established standards for a good care policy—including Alzheimer's coverage, inflation protection, no prior hospitalization requirement, etc.

Most states have adopted all or some of the NAIC proposals. Effective January 1992, for example, New York State requires insurers to pay for Alzheimer's, and places a 6-month maximum on periods of nonpayment for pre-existing conditions. Other states, including California and Connecticut, are becoming, or may become, partners with insurers to offer long-term care insurance. By doing this, these states hope to reduce state Medicaid payments. On the federal level, many experts expect to see broad legislation regarding this issue in the near future.

How can a senior decide if he or she needs these pricy policies? The answer depends on income, his or her family support network, and other factors, but the numbers seem to indicate that these policies may be a good idea. Fully 22% of all Americans age 85 and older reside in nursing homes. Yet the policies are also risky: Unlike life insurance, long-term care insurance doesn't guarantee the insured or his or her family will ever collect anything.

## REAL-LIFE TIP

If you can, wait to buy a long-term care insurance policy until new consumer protection laws make shopping easier. Other issues, such as whether premiums are tax-deductible and whether benefits are tax-free, may also be resolved.

# Options I: Home Care

No segment of the booming eldercare industry is growing faster than home care. There are 12,500 profit and not-for-profit home care enterprises in the country today—1,500 of which were launched in 1990 alone.

Why the great appeal of home care? The main reasons are:

HOME SWEET HOME
A full 86% of senior citizens want to stay at home—"aging in place," as the sociologists call it.

GOOD MEDICINE
Several studies show that people generally heal more quickly, live longer, and are happier at home than in hospitals or nursing homes.

CHEAP TOO!
According to a 1987 study, recuperating after surgery will cost a hospital patient or his or her insurer $300 to $500 a day or more. Home care costs can be a small fraction of that, and they compare favorably with nursing home costs too.

INSURER INTEREST
Insurers who formerly spurned home care coverage have begun to embrace it as news of its affordability has spread. Medicare, for example, will spring for home care

(but only if the recipient is homebound, needs skilled nursing care or speech therapy, and satisfies certain other criteria). Long-term care insurance often covers home care too. *Bottom line*: Insurer coverage of home health care is spotty, but growing.

CHANGES IN PAYMENTS

In 1983, Medicare began to pay only a fixed amount to hospitals, based on the patient's illness. Formerly, payments were determined by length of stay. The new fixed-fee schemes encouraged hospitals to get patients out fast—giving a boost to home care.

HIGH TECH AT HOME

Advances in medical technology—particularly in the portability of various machines—have expanded the range of treatments people can now receive at home. Examples: Kidney dialysis and oxygen therapy are now easily administered at home.

What are the segments of the sizable and growing home care industry? There are three: Home Services, provided by a growing array of professionals and nonprofessionals; Home Adaptations, architectural and technological, that make seniors' home life convenient and worry-free; and Special Housing Arrangements that provide seniors with safety and comfort.

## 1. Home Services: Cast of Thousands

The home visit is the central act of home care, and the cast of home visitors is growing along with the industry.

Depending on the senior's regimen, home care visitors may include doctors, registered nurses, licensed practical nurses, occupational therapists, physical therapists, psychologists, social workers, nutritionists, health aides, homemakers, and more.

## BEWARE: REAL DANGERS

Home health care is little regulated in some states. The federal government has some rules, but they only apply to Medicare-certified agencies—a minority in the home care industry. Thirty-nine states have some licensing rules, but most only pertain to skilled nursing agencies.

The upshot: There's great opportunity for fraud and abuse in home care. When hiring aides and agencies, ask for credentials and references and check them thoroughly.

In many communities, there are regular home service programs for transportation, home repair, and so on—often offered through churches, senior centers, and social service agencies. Among the most popular are:

A. MEALS ON WHEELS
Nutritious meals are delivered several or more days each week to those unable to shop or cook for themselves. These delivered meals are often subsidized.

## B. HOME VISITORS

Often, churches or community groups will dispatch volunteers or paid workers to visit the homebound elderly on a regular basis, both to provide companionship and to check that all is well.

## C. TELEPHONE REASSURANCE

These are monitoring programs in which police, church, or community volunteers either make or receive calls from the elderly each day. A missed call prompts a home visit.

A big question is who will coordinate this potentially large cast of home helpers. With the exception of certain states, including New York, that require full case management of all its certified home health agencies and long-term home health care programs, the answer is usually the family caregiver. But now, caregivers, especially distant or very busy ones, have an option. They can hire a surrogate called a care manager or case manager.

These professionals—often experienced social workers—will typically draft a plan for fulfilling the needs of the elderly person and implement and monitor that plan as well, hiring health care agencies and homemakers, securing transportation for the homebound, and assisting in nursing home placement, if necessary. The initial plan may cost $150 to $500, with hourly fees for further work ranging from $40 to $125. There are public care managers too, who may be cheaper or even free.

**REAL-LIFE TIP**

For listings of public and private care managers in your area, call the National Association of Private Geriatric Care Managers (602-881-8008) and the National Association of Area Agencies on Aging (202-296-8130).

## 2. Adapting the Home

Just as a home can be "childproofed" for your toddler, it can also be adapted for the aging. One of the most important adaptations is a PERS—Personal Emergency Response System.

Introduced in the mid-1970s and sold under such names as Lifeline, Lifewatch, and Voice of Help, PERS are simply signaling devices. If an elderly person living alone needs emergency help, he or she would push the PERS call button he or she carries in a pocket or on a necklace. The signal is transmitted through a console on the telephone to the police, ambulance service, or the PERS manufacturer's own monitors.

PERS are not cheap—they can run as much as $200 to $1,000 to start with, and a $15 to $30 monthly monitoring fee. NOTE: Installation of a PERS may be free or subsidized through a local hospital or Office of Aging.

## SENIOR-SCAM ALERT

Beware! Some PERS firms prey on the elderly, using high-pressure sales tactics and selling unworkable or overpriced units. One company was even found to be providing nothing more than a call to your local 911—for $30 a month. Before buying, check with your state's consumer protection agency.

Other home adaptations—some high-tech, some low-tech and some just common-sense—include:

- *Double-Faced Adhesive Tape* on rugs to prevent falls.
- *Kickplates* on doors so the wheelchair-bound can open them.
- *Grab Bars* on the bathtub wall for steadying.
- *Levers* rather than knobs on doors and drawers for ease of use by arthritic hands.
- *Widened Doorways* for wheelchair access.
- *Automatic Operators* for heavy or cumbersome doors or drawers.

Only the imagination limits these alterations, and first-hand experience with a senior's troubles in the house is the best source of ideas. (TRY THIS: A mirror above the stove can help the wheelchair-bound to see if the stew is cooked.)

One excellent source on home adaptation: *The DoAble Renewable Home*, available from the AARP (202-872-4700). Be aware, too, that when retirees move to Florida or Arizona or some other retirement spot, they should ask to see homes with adaptations for the elderly.

## 3. Special Housing: Is There an *ECHO* in Here?

As the popularity of PERS proves, living alone can bring with it great fears for seniors. Add the need for companionship and help around the house, and there is a clear desire for seniors to live either with, or very close to, someone. Here are three typical solutions:

### A. MOVE IN WITH THE KIDS

Sixty percent of seniors move in with their children for at least a while. Kickplates and levers and other adaptations can always be made, but the emotional adaptations are often much harder. Such arrangements are often happy, of course, but there's plenty of room for stress and tension among grandparents, parents, spouses, and children. Some tips:

- Watch out for resumption of old roles.
- Have clear divisions of labor and authority.
- Maintain routines.

For an excellent bibliography on the relationship of adult children and aging parents, call Children of Aging Parents (CAPS) at 215-945-6900.

## REAL-LIFE TAX TIP

Do you pay someone to take care of an aging relative? Many people try to take medical deductions for these costs on their tax returns, but you can only do so if total unreimbursed medical expenses exceed 7.5% of your adjusted gross income. BETTER IDEA: You may be eligible for a dependent care credit, which is not subject to the 7.5% limit, and unlike a deduction, reduces your taxes dollar for dollar.

## B. BRING IN A BOARDER

For companionship and some help with home expenses, some elderly rent a room or more to an unrelated person. Now called "homesharing," this is simply the old practice of taking in a boarder. But remember, under any name, it carries the same dangers of frictions due to incompatible lifestyles. Another option is for a senior or his family to hire a professional, live-in companion. That option can be expensive, however.

## C. ACCESSORIES AND ECHOS

Some seniors can manage to have privacy without living alone. A spacious mansion would do the trick, but there are two more realistic approaches:

*Accessory Apartments.* When it's architectually feasible, some seniors can create separate, self-contained living units within a larger residence. Whether the other occupants are family or not, and whoever owns the structure, this arrangement can provide the safety and pleasure of nearby companions—and solitude too.

*ECHO Housing.* **E**lder **C**ottage **H**ousing **O**pportunity cottages are small, portable, cheap ($25,000) living units that enable aging parents to live in detached units on the grounds of their children's homes. Usually having two bedrooms and inspired by Australian "granny flats," ECHO units are specifically designed for the elderly and disabled. NOTE: You may need a zoning variance or special-use permit for ECHO in your town—check with your town's zoning board.

For more information on this subject, call the AARP for *"Your Home, Your Choice"* (202-872-4700).

## Options II: Community Resources

Seniors living at home or with relatives can spend limited amounts of time at various community sites for care and companionship. Listed below are the major drop-in sites and other facilities found in many areas:

## 1. Senior Centers

Mainly intended for mobile and independent elderly persons, senior centers are places to eat, play, and socialize. Often run by churches and other not-for-profit institutions, these centers can also function as community clearinghouses for information about senior services. Some centers provide transportation to and from the site; others furnish companions for their visitors. Most don't charge for their services.

## 2. Adult Day Care

There are more than 2,500 adult day care centers operating today, and they range from social clubs similar to the senior centers mentioned above, to medically oriented facilities which offer occupational therapy, physical and speech therapy, nursing supervision, etc. Run by nursing homes, not-for-profit groups, or local agencies, day care centers also offer valuable relief for a caregiver who must go to work or simply needs a break.

Fees can average about $30 a day or more depending on the nature of the services provided, but some centers are free or subsidized while others charge on a sliding scale pegged to income. Adult day care is not usually covered by Medicare, Medigap, or private health insurance, but it may be covered under Medicaid and long-term care insurance. Transportation is usually provided.

## 3. Respite Care

This service can be offered in the home, a nursing facility, or an adult day care center, but the aim is always the same: caregiver relief. With respite care, caregivers who are overwhelmed, ill, traveling on business or pleasure, or otherwise unable to provide care to a senior can be "spelled" for a brief time, from several hours to several days.

The care is often free, particularly when it's furnished

by volunteers from local churches or groups. Medicaid and long-term care insurance may provide some coverage if the service is not free.

## 4. Hospice Care

These programs provide care for the terminally ill, emphasizing home care and family involvement in the process of dying. This growing movement—1,700 hospices helped 190,000 people and their families in 1988—stresses pain relief rather than curative care.

Typically, hospice staff members will train family members to bathe and medicate the patient, make occasional home visits, and monitor care. Hospices also offer bereavement programs for families.

Hospice costs range from $50 to $400 per day and insurance coverage generally helps. Medicare, for example, covers up to 210 days of care, provided there is a diagnosis of a terminal illness. Private health insurance often has hospice benefits too, though mainly in group workplace plans. Long-term care insurance may also pay for this care.

*Caution*: Hospices are young and their regulation and standards of care are still evolving. Yet, half the nation's hospices are Medicare-certified, and more than half the states license these facilities. Many are also accredited by the Joint Commission on the Accreditation of Health Care Organizations (312-642-6061).

For a good idea of what constitutes quality hospice

care, call the National Hospice Organization (703-243-5900) and ask for its list of basic hospice principles.

## REAL-LIFE TIP

Community services for the aging vary enormously from town to town. To get a quick fix on your area's offerings, consult churches, community groups, social service agencies, state and local offices for the aging, and senior centers. There's also a National Hospice Hotline (800-658-8898) for hospices in your region, and the Silver Pages Directory, which lists business discounts and free community services for seniors nationwide (800-252-6060).

# Options III: Home Away From Home

However valiantly a family tries, it may be impossible to keep a senior at home. The often-wrenching decision to move is made tougher by the cost and complexity of the housing decision. The good news: There are growing numbers of high-quality housing choices for the elderly, ranging from rooming houses with only minimal services to full-fledged nursing homes with round-the-clock medical supervision.

Below is a brief glossary of these options, roughly in ascending order of cost and medical care. For more information on senior housing, call the American Association of Homes for the Aging (202-296-5960) or the National Consumers League (202-639-8140) as well as your state associations.

## 1. Adult Homes

Also called senior apartments, old age homes, adult care facilities, and apartments for independent living, adult homes are geared toward those basically healthy seniors who don't want to or can't live alone or shoulder all the burdens of housekeeping. Adult home residents have private quarters of one to three rooms, and enjoy complete independence. They may share several or more meals a week, and basic light housekeeping is provided. In some cases and subject to certain limitations, adult homes will furnish assistance with bathing or dressing or with medical care. They may, however, provide transportation to stores, doctor's offices, and so on.

Adult homes charge a monthly fee, comparable to local rents, plus fees for meals and other provided services. Medicare, Medigap, and private insurance generally will not pay for this type of care, which may be provided by not-for-profit, for-profit, or public organizations.

Some adult homes are designed with the elderly in mind. Apartments may have intercoms to a central office for emergencies, and electric outlets may be placed high on walls to avoid difficult bending.

**REAL-LIFE TIP**

When searching for an adult home, ask to stay a day to see what it's like—or at least sample a meal with the other residents.

## 2. Congregate Housing

These facilities are adult homes on a larger scale, usually 50 to 150 units in a building, with a central dining room, private apartments, and shared living spaces. Like other adult homes, the staff may include a nutritionist, social director, and housekeepers.

## 3. Board and Care Homes

Also called rest homes or personal-care homes, these facilities cater to seniors who are mostly healthy and alert, but need minor assistance with daily tasks.

While congregate housing residents often do their own laundry, "B&Cs" often have staff to handle that and other chores. Also, B&C residents often take all their meals together, while their adult home counterparts do so just occasionally. B&Cs vary from place to place, though: 34% of them assist residents with eating, and 88% clean residents' private rooms.

Usually sited in large private houses—like the boarding homes from which they took their name—B&Cs are typically Mom and Pop operations with fewer than thirty residents. States license and inspect these homes only spottily, and many owners have neglected to license their homes.

In all, there are 30,000 to 50,000 B&Cs sheltering 600,000 to 800,000 elderly. Medicaid and long-term care insurance may pay some B&C costs.

*Home Hunter Tips:* Most B&Cs are private, for-profit ventures which, like adult homes, charge a monthly fee for rent and services. Often operating with no public supervision, B&C owners can and sometimes do defraud the elderly. Here are four ways to safeguard your senior:

A. KNOW WHAT YOU'RE PAYING FOR

Get a detailed cost breakdown. What is the monthly fee? (It ranges from $240 to $1,200.) What services are included in the fee? For services billed separately, what are the costs?

B. NEGOTIATE A LEASE

B&C homes are essentially rentals, their owners landlords. To protect your senior, get a lease.

C. CHECK THE CHECKBOOK

Many B&C operators manage their residents' funds, a practice that permits much abuse. Help your senior monitor his or her own money.

D. TOUR AND TALK

Never join a B&C without touring it—preferably without supervision—and talking at length to residents. Be sure to check the home for cleanliness, any odors, and pleasant surroundings.

## 4. Assisted Living Facilities

These residences serve the same clientele as B&C homes—frail but fundamentally healthy seniors—and provide the same kind of minimal custodial care. The difference: They are corporate, not Mom and Pop, operations, and they're bigger than B&Cs. The Hyatt Hotel organization, for example, is opening a chain of assisted living facilities called Classic Residences. Other companies are also interested. For those wary of the risks of Mom and Pop B&Cs, this new housing alternative may be worth investigating.

## 5. Continuing Care Retirement Communities

CCRCs—also related to so-called life-care communities (LCCs)—are a creative, expensive, and risky new option for seniors. With roots in nineteenth century religious communities, CCRCs are virtually all not-for-profit. But enterprises like the Marriott Hotel chain are showing interest.

It's no wonder. CCRCs and LCCs are the fastest-growing segment of the elderly-housing industry. Two hundred and fifty thousand seniors live in 700 CCRCs and LCCs today, and those numbers are expected to double by the year 2000.

CCRCs provide a continuum of care—from independent living to twenty-four-hour nursing services—in one setting. Residents buy into an LCC for life, but they can rest assured that they will always be cared for, whenever and however their health may deteriorate (but subject to the contract limits noted below).

CCRC and LCC physical sites are often as extensive as their services. Their campuses can include private apartments, recreational facilities, dining hall, nursing home, and more.

The cost for all this is high. CCRCs and LCCs charge a one-time entrance fee that can range from $27,000 to a whopping $325,000 (depending on the size and quality of the facility, the size of the resident's apartment, and the nursing home provisions in the resident's contract, and other factors). Then comes the monthly fee, typically between $600 and $3,500. Worse: These costs are not reimbursable under Medicare or private health insurance. What's more, these charges usually don't purchase the elderly person any equity: The entry fee simply buys a contract for lifetime care.

Not all CCRC and LCC contracts are equal, however. There are three basic varieties—and their differences all center on nursing home care:

TYPE A
This all-inclusive contract guarantees lifetime nursing home care—as long as the resident makes his or her monthly payments.

TYPE B
This modified plan provides CCRC residents with a fixed number of days of free nursing home care, either each

year or for life. If the "free" days are exhausted, the resident pays extra—but less than market rates.

## TYPE C

Under this contract, residents pay for nursing home care as they need it. Some CCRCs require those electing this plan to carry long-term care insurance.

Judging from their rapid growth, CCRCs fill seniors' deeply felt need for lifelong security of housing and health care. But there's a big problem. CCRCs can survive financially only if they guess right about how long residents will live and how much expensive nursing care they'll need. Many guess wrong. One study of 50 CCRCs found that between 1980 and 1985, 10% defaulted on their debts. Residents of bankrupt CCRCs may lose their entry fees with little recourse.

To make matters worse, there's little government oversight of these communities. Federal agencies don't supervise CCRCs at all, and while two-thirds of the states do have regulations, they usually just require CCRCs to make full financial disclosure to prospective residents.

For these reasons, CCRC shoppers should verify a facility's financial soundness while also evaluating its costs and services:

- *Ask* what the community's financial reserves are, and whether it is financially independent.
- *Obtain* the CCRC's audited financial records, and take them to an accountant for expert analysis.

## REAL-LIFE TIP

Beware! According to the Federal Trade Commission, the religious heritage of CCRCs has led some unscrupulous operators to claim that they have the financial support of an established church. This may be true—and it may not. Get it in writing.

## 6. Nursing Homes

Approximately 2.3 million elderly, frail, and disabled Americans live in nursing homes, and millions more will be joining them soon. These homes offer a wide range of nursing, therapeutic, custodial, and recreational services. Residents may only be admitted on a physician's order, and a registered nurse must be on duty during every daytime shift. Residents may require primarily custodial care, or intermediate or skilled nursing care.

Annual charges for nursing homes run from $25,000 to $70,000+ per year. Typically, residents will exhaust their savings on the home's bills, and then go on Medicaid. This picture may change, though. The recent upsurge in long-term care insurance may eventually make insurers a primary payor of nursing home charges.

Nursing homes must follow federal and state rules. To get Medicare and Medicaid payments, for example, homes must observe a residents' "Bill of Rights" that makes their quality of life a major priority and protects them from invasions of privacy, unnecessary use of wrist straps and other restraints, etc.

State licensing rules go beyond the federal guidelines. For homes that don't participate in Medicare and Medicaid, states provide the only outside monitoring. But such monitoring can be spotty: In California a few years ago, only 14.3% of $32.4 million in fines assessed against nursing homes was ever collected. Why? A lack of staffing and resources has made it difficult to adequately monitor the industry.

The lesson here is to let the buyer beware. There are many shocking instances of fraud and abuse in nursing homes: unanswered call bells, sedation of residents for staff convenience, and staff theft of residents' property. Less dramatic, but just as damaging, is the pervasiveness of poor-quality care. A leading nursing home reformer says only 30% of homes provide "very good care." Here are some tips to protect your loved one from these dangers:

A. NOT-FOR-PROFIT PREFERRED?

There are good for-profit nursing homes, especially the high-price variety. But in some cases, not-for-profits outperform the profits. Whichever type you are considering, be certain to evaluate the facility's ratings by state and federal agencies.

B. RIGHT RATIOS

Staff size: A ratio of at least one staffer to every two residents is a good guide.

C. ASK THE OMBUDSMAN

Federal law requires that every state have at least one full-time ombudsman to monitor nursing homes and protect residents. *Always* call your ombudsman to find out the record of homes that interest you. Is the home's license in order? Is it Medicare-certified? Has it been the subject of any complaints?

D. MAKE SEVERAL SURPRISE VISITS

Visit the nursing home several times, at different times of the day and the week. Make at least some visits unannounced.

E. LOOK AND LEARN

Observe the home's environment. Are there handrails in the halls, grab bars in the bathrooms? Are there unsteady chairs? Is the place clean and neat? Do the residents and staff seem open, engaged, happy?

F. RESPECT FOR RESIDENTS

How high is the regard for residents? Is there a residents' council that meets regularly? Can residents decorate their own rooms? Do residents have a say in roommate assignments? Can residents retain their own private physicians?

G. FUN AND GAMES

What social and recreational facilities does the home have? Is there a full-time social director? Are there trips to museums, libraries, films? Is there a good variety of in-house activities—bingo, parties, outside speakers?

H. MEDICAL MATTERS

To what hospital are residents taken? Is there a doctor on call twenty-four hours for emergencies? Is the director of nursing an RN? Will specialists—dentists, optometrists—make housecalls? Are there good programs for physical and occupational therapy?

# 6 $ 🏠 🚗 ⛽ ♥

# Investing in the 1990s

### "If You Still Have Any Money Left"

**Y**ou work hard for your money. So hard, in fact, that you probably don't have the time, energy, or ability to manage and invest your money in any effective way. What's more, you probably don't have much of the green stuff to invest anyway, and the people on Wall Street speak what sounds like a foreign language with terms like "futures indexes" and "price-earnings ratios" being thrown around like food at a college frat party.

Despite these hurdles, the lesson to be learned from this chapter is that it doesn't make sense to work hard for your money if you don't take the time and effort to make sure that your money works hard for you. This means, first of all, minimizing the interest you pay on your mortgage and credit cards and, on the other side of the investment equation, earning the best return on your invested money. So, whether you're "well-heeled" or virtually "shoeless," you should do *something*.

And do it now, because the earlier you start, the easier it will be. One example: If you start saving to send your child to a private college when she's ten, you'll need to squirrel away a whopping $906 a month to pay for her tuition and expenses—OUCH! But, if you begin when she's still wearing diapers, say about two years old, your monthly requirement drops to about $538—little ouch! For a state school, you'd have to save about $430 and $256, respectively.

Investing wisely has always been important. But it's even more critical for us, today's adults—Baby Boomers and Busters if you insist—most of whom face a less optimistic financial future than our parents. For one thing, our homes, if we can ever put together the down payment to buy one, will never experience the gains in value that were seen during the 1950s and on through the 1980s. And with Social Security headed toward the intensive care ward, and pension funds facing increasing trouble, many experts say that we will need to find at least an extra $100,000 to pay for even a moderately comfortable retirement.

This chapter discusses the ins and outs of this increasingly vital subject, from the merits of mutual funds to the warning signs of stock scams. We'll also go through a step-by-step guide to making our money work as hard as we do, including specific tactics for handling two of life's most daunting financial hurdles: college tuition (your children's) and retirement (your own).

## Rule One: Try to Save Something

Virtually all of us should invest, and can. You may think you're stretched to the limit, but there are ways to scrounge up some money. What about that long-forgotten passbook savings account? Or why not save $25 from each week's paycheck for a few months? How about that income tax refund you got last month? You don't need much to get started.

But wait! Investing your money may be premature. Don't put away any of your money until you've satisfied a few basic needs. The basics include:

- Food, clothing, and shelter.
- Adequate life, health, and disability insurance.
- An emergency fund of at least six months of income—more if your job security is on the ropes.

## Compare Your Income and Your Outgo

Let's say that you just got an income tax refund of $500. Great! But don't board the next train to Wall Street just yet. True, stocks may be earning 12% (at the moment), but what about those credit card balances of yours? That's right, the ones costing you 18%. Your $500 will earn $60 a year at the stock market's 12% pace. But if you pay off your credit card bill instead, you'll save yourself $90 in nondeductible interest payments.

*Moral*: Sometimes it's smarter to pay off your debts than to invest. The first thing I tried to do after finishing graduate school was to start repaying my student loans, some of which were costing me 16%! Unfortunately, these interest-rate comparisons are not always so cut and dry. Some examples:

## 1. The Tax Factor

A 12% mortgage actually costs you less than 12% because the interest portion of the payments is tax-deductible. How much less depends on your tax bracket (and the percentage of your mortgage payment that's paying for the interest of the loan and not its principal). If you pay about 33% of your income in taxes, for example, your mortgage interest is costing you about 8%.

## 2. Prepayment Penalties

Some loans have prepayment penalties (usually only during the first year) that make early repayment unwise— even when the interest you are paying is relatively high.

## 3. New Home Loans?

When interest rates drop, many homeowners move to refinance their high-interest mortgages. But the costs of refinancing, with its "points" and other closing costs, can run you several thousand dollars. One long-standing rule says that you shouldn't refinance unless the new mortgage rate is at least 2% lower than your old one and you plan to stay in the home at least five more years.

Of course, real life is more complex than that. To figure out if refinancing makes sense, you'll have to crunch a bunch of numbers, including your old and new interest rates, the closing costs on the new loan, and how long you plan to stay in your home (ask your banker to help).

---

# Learn About Credit

---

"**N**either a borrower nor a lender be." Shakespeare may still run on Broadway, but this advice from the Bard is repeatedly ignored by modern man. In our defense, readily available credit is everywhere to tempt us: mortgages, bank cards, personal loans, department-store cards, etc. Problem: Few of us have the required discipline to handle credit or even understand the basics of shopping for credit. Here's what you need to know.

## 1. Annual Percentage Rate (APR)
This measures the total interest cost of the extended credit. Unlike the interest rate, the APR factors in the frequency of repayment.

## 2. Finance Charge
This is the total cost of the credit—the APR plus service charges, annual fees, mortgage points, etc.

Federal laws require all creditors, from banks to department stores, to inform you of the APR and the finance charge on loans. These truth-in-lending laws guarantee that borrowers can easily compare different loan options.

That's good, because borrowers should do a lot of comparing. There's no federal ceiling on credit costs, and no regulations exist in about one-quarter of the states. And the ceiling in states that do have regulations can reach 30% or more. Whether you're looking for a car loan or a credit card, make sure to shop around. And whatever doubletalk the sales reps try to hand you, keep your eye on the prize: the APR and the finance charges.

*Note to spendthrifts*: Credit is valuable, and expensive. Use it sparingly. If you can, pay your credit card bill(s) promptly and in full each month to avoid any finance charges. Also, keep your debt level manageable (between 36–42% of gross income, including your home, is recommended).

---

## REAL-LIFE TIPS

Smart move: Take out a home equity loan, which typically has both low interest and tax-deductibility, and use the money to pay off your credit cards and other debts that have no tax breaks and charge interest in the teens. The average family can save $700 a year this way. WARNING: In order to get a tax deduction on your home equity loan you will need to itemize your deductions on your tax return—ask your accountant. Tip 2: Try refinancing your bank credit cards as well. You can often just transfer your old balance to your new low-interest card.

---

## A Stash For Your Ready Cash

Great! You're provided for your living expenses and certain important needs like life insurance. You've also minimized your credit costs, and you've socked away at least 6 months of salary for emergencies. You've got your $500 tax refund, and, by saving some of each week's paycheck,

and missing a few meals out each month, you've saved a
few thousand more. You're ready to quit your job and install that Dow Jones ticker tape in your den ...

Wait just a second, J. P. Morgan! Before buying any
stocks and bonds, you need a place, a parking lot if you
will, to put your operating money for monthly expenses.
You need to keep these funds liquid (available quickly)
and safe. In stormy times, you may also want to use
your parking lot as a safe haven for your investment
money.

These requirements don't mean you can't also earn
some interest on this money, however. This is especially
true since bank deregulation in the 1980s spurred competition in new customer services. Here are two of the most
popular "parking lots" for your cash:

## 1. How "NOW" Brown Cow?

A NOW (Negotiable Order of Withdrawal) account is a
checking account that earns interest. But it only earns interest if you maintain a minimum balance; sink below the
minimum and the bank will charge you for maintenance
of the account and your check writing. When shopping
for a good NOW account, don't be dazzled by high rates.
Ask about the minimums and fees. Also ask if different
accounts can be linked together to satisfy the minimum
balance requirement. Check if the fees are charged if the
account falls below the minimum for as little as one day
during the month or only if your average monthly balance falls below the minimum (the second option is obviously better).

## 2. Money Market Funds

Invented in 1972, money market funds have grown in popularity. These funds invest in CDs, Treasury bills, and other "moneylike" instruments, either on a taxable or tax-free basis. Run either by banks or mutual funds, these accounts pay changing rates of interest, are very liquid, and offer check-writing privileges. The bank and mutual fund versions of money market funds have some differences:

- Bank funds are federally insured up to $100,000. Those offered by mutual funds are not, but they're still generally very safe.
- Mutual fund money market accounts often have check-writing minimums of $250 or $500. Those offered by banks may limit the number of checks that you can write each month—usually three—but not their size.
- Bank fund interest rates may change monthly, or even more frequently, while mutual fund rates always change daily.

### REAL INTEREST

Not all equal interest rates are equal. There's simple interest and compound interest, and the second can be calculated annually, quarterly, or daily. These differences affect your return: A 5.25% savings account earns 5.25% if it's compounded annually, but 5.47% if it's compounded daily. A simple way to get to the bottom line: Ask for the *effective annual yield*, which incorporates these different calculation methods.

# "Where Is My Money Safe?"

We've all heard about the many recent failures in the financial industry. But don't put your money in the mattress just yet. There are many safety nets that protect your money even if your bank or other institution goes under.

## 1. Banks

Only use banks that offer protection for your deposits under FDIC—the Federal Deposit Insurance Corporation. With FDIC protection, your accounts up to $100,000 are protected.

## 2. Insurance Companies

Some have gone under, and more probably will in the future. In most cases, state governments have bailed out customers, but your best bet is to invest only with the safest companies in the industry. For more on picking a safe insurance company see chapter 4.

## 3. Credit Unions

These institutions are playing an expanding role in the investment industry. Look for credit unions that insure depositers through the National Credit Union Share Insurance Fund (NCUSIF). Others may be insured by state agencies, but repayment in the case of failure can be time-consuming.

# Hitting the Street (Wall Street)

Now that you're ready to invest, you need to know about your investment alternatives. "The Street" calls them "investment vehicles"—a good metaphor for their underlying characteristics. Some of the vehicles—like growth stocks—are speedy. They'll take your money farther, faster, but they also have a greater chance of crashing. Others—like CDs—are slow. They're less likely to crash, but they won't rack up fast profits either. In other words, the greater, or less, the risk, the greater, or less, the potential rewards.

The mode of transportation that's right for you depends on your stage in life, your tolerance for risk, your family situation, and other factors. Here's a guided tour through the investment vehicles showroom:

## 1. CDs

(No, not compact discs!) Certificates of deposit are very conservative investments offered by banks. Their main disadvantage is their lack of liquidity: You must agree to leave your money untouched for a certain period of time, or suffer what the banks call "substantial penalties for early withdrawal."

CD terms range from one month to ten years. Their interest rates are usually fixed, so buying CDs is a guessing game: Which way will interest rates go? If you think that rates will fall, for example, you'll want to choose a long-term CD to "lock-in" today's high rates. If your crystal ball is sighting heavy inflation, you'll probably want to buy a short-term CD so you can reinvest your money as rates move higher.

*Best Strategy:* If you're investing in CDs, "ladder" your investments by buying CDs with different maturities to take advantage of changing rates and investment alternatives.

---

### REAL-LIFE TIP

CD rates vary greatly from region to region, so it pays to shop beyond just the banks in your town. This may sound difficult, but it's actually very easy to do. *Money* magazine and most major newspapers regularly list the banks (and their 800 numbers) that are currently offering the highest yields on CDs. But remember, given the recent bank failures, never invest more than the insured amount.

---

## 2. Stocks

The basic, best investment. Stocks make you an owner of a corporation. Your return is determined both by dividends—profits paid out periodically to shareholders— and any appreciation in the price of the stock. Stocks come in every size, shape, and color. There are risky stocks, safe stocks, foreign stocks, big-company stocks, small-company stocks, penny stocks, high price-per-share stocks, and on and on.

How can you tell if a stock is a good buy? That's the question on which Wall Street careers are made or broken. The answers are many, both technical and intuitive.

Some analysts look for good buys by comparing price-to-book-value ratios or price-earnings multiples. Others simply buy shares in Waste Management because they sometimes mistakenly think that there's going to be more garbage and toxic waste to be collected. Some analysts even use the Super Bowl outcome (an NFL victory indicates to them higher near-term prices) and next year's hemlines (up means down, or is it down means up?) to help them try to get rich. The one indisputable fact is that stocks rise and fall with the fortunes of the individual company, the industry as a whole, the economy of the country, and even the world's economy.

## 3. Bonds

To buy a bond is to actually make a loan to some entity. There are corporate bonds issued by companies, Treasury bonds issued by the federal government, and municipal bonds sold by states and localities. Public agencies issue bonds too, some with names straight out of *Gone With the Wind*—Fannie Mae and Ginnie Mae. Perhaps the best-known bonds are U.S. Savings Bonds, a favorite among small investors.

Bonds are generally less risky than stocks. But some bonds—such as junk bonds—are very risky, while others—such as U.S. government bonds—are quite safe. Like stocks, bonds can be bought through brokers and mutual funds; though some bonds, like Treasury bonds, can be bought directly from the issuer.

Unlike stocks, many bonds carry tax advantages. Federal government bonds, for example, are exempt from state and local taxes, and municipal bonds are free from federal taxes and taxes in the issuing state.

---

### TAX TIP

Can't decide between a taxable investment and a tax-free one? There's a simple way to compare. Give your tax bracket to the sales rep who's offering you the tax-free deal and he or she will be able to give you the taxable equivalent yield (TEY) of the investment. The TEY tells you the return necessary on a taxable investment to equal, after taxes, the return on the tax-free one.

---

That's it. There are other investments you can make—gold; collectibles like art, stamps, and coins; limited partnerships; stock options; and commodity futures in lard or soybeans, to name just a few. But the investment vehicles described above are the basics for your ride on the road to riches. The next question: Who's going to drive?

## Investment Basics

At this point, you may be asking the following question: "Since I know as much about price-earnings ratios and commodity futures as I do about nuclear weaponry, is there any guidance for me out there? Anybody I can trust?" The good news: Yes there is, as we will discuss below. The bad news: Even if you do get help, you'll still need to familiarize yourself with the basics of investing in order to monitor your investments and your "trusted" helper. How many stories have we all heard about investment advisers who, after gaining the confidence of a client, have fled to Pago Pago with their client's hard-earned money?

Good news, again: The basics of investing are not as complex as you think:

## 1. Don't Put All Your Eggs in One Basket

Sounds trite but this is the first rule of investing, to which Wall Streeters have given the fancy name of "portfolio diversification." While the term may be hard to pronounce, the concept is easy:

- It means investing in not just one investment vehicle but in all of them. Though recent events have cast some doubt on this principle, the conventional wisdom is that when stocks go up bonds go down and vice versa. Having both is the classic method of avoiding risk. Unfortunately, it also limits your potential for large gains.
- It means investing in not just one company, but in several, at least.
- It means investing in different sectors of the economy. Suppose you adhere to Rule B and buy several stocks. If they're all chocolate-chip cookie companies, you'll be in hot milk if the government all of a sudden issued a health warning linking excessive chocolate-chip cookie consumption with cancer.
- It means investing in international economies as well as the United States. Fully two-thirds of the

world's stock is issued in countries other than the
United States.

## 2. Divide Up Your Dollars

The mix-it-up message is pretty obvious, but how do you
do this? How much of your $5,000 in investment funds,
for example, should go to stocks? To bonds? etc.? How
much to risky growth stocks, and how much to safer income stocks? Basically, this simply means dividing up the
pie, but again the Street has a phrase for it: "asset allocation."

Two lessons are important here. First, there are no
definite answers. In late 1991, the *Wall Street Journal*
asked several respected brokerage houses—Shearson,
Prudential, etc.—to recommend asset mixes for a hypo-
thetical thirtysomething single parent. The experts' answers ranged from 18% to 66% in growth stocks. So much
for the science of finance.

Lesson 2: Despite Lesson #1, there are generally
agreed asset-allocation principles. Some main ones include:

### A. STICK WITH STOCKS

Over the long haul, stocks outperform all other investment vehicles. From 1972 to 1989, for example, stocks
earned an average annual return of 11.4%. They should
be your core investment.

## B. YOUNG AND RISKY, OLD AND SAFE

The younger you are the more investment risk you can take. Reason: You have more time to ride out market fluctuations.

## C. ANALYZE YOUR GOALS

What are you investing for? Kids' college? House? Car down payment? Retirement? The closer the goal, the more conservative your investment strategy should be.

## D. KNOW YOUR RISK TOLERANCE LEVEL

People are different. Some of us can sleep tight with our life savings riding on a speculative growth stock. Others can't relax—even with their money in AT&T. Stay within your "risk comfort" zone—you'll sleep better.

The best way to allocate assets is to draw a pie chart and play around with slices of different sizes for different investment vehicles. There's plenty of help available. *Barron's, Money, Forbes*, and the *Wall Street Journal* all regularly run such asset-allocation charts.

Is it worth it? The answer is a definite YES! Many investors spend a lot of their time agonizing over which is the hot stock or mutual fund. But studies have shown that 80% of investment earnings are determined not by those decisions but by the allocation of assets among stocks, bonds, certificates of deposit, and money market funds.

## 3. Schedule Your Buys And Sells

You'll love the Wall Street–ese for this one: "dollar cost averaging." The idea is simple. No one knows if and when the stock market will go up or down. The strategy: Buy constant-dollar amounts of stocks over regular intervals. With your $5,000, for example, you might invest $500 every five weeks or so for about one year. Your $500 will buy more shares when prices are low, and fewer shares when prices are high.

The experts (who are these experts anyway?) claim that you'll get a reasonable average price using this method. And you won't go crazy if you invest your entire $5,000 at the market peak—a favorite strategy of mine—only to watch your investment fall hopelessly.

When you sell you do the same thing, only with constant-*share* amounts rather than constant-dollar amounts. The only drawback to this practice is that you'll end up paying higher commissions on your smaller, and more frequent, transactions. One way around this problem is to invest through mutual funds.

## 4. Stick It Out

This is the simplest rule of investing, and the hardest to follow. The idea: Stocks are volatile in the short term but not over longer periods of time. The market may fall 120 points or even 500 points in a single bleak day, but over the years it will gradually climb ever upward, earning you a nice return on your patience. So only invest money you won't need for a while. And stick it out.

## Should You Use A Financial Planner?

Investment fundamentals may seem relatively straightforward, but things can get dicey. There may be complex questions of taxes, insurance, pensions, estate planning, accounting, and so on. Asset allocation is no snap either. Do you need a guide—a financial planner—to lead you through the caverns of investing?

The answer for you may be yes, or it may be no. Here are the factors that might lead you to go it alone:

- Your finances are relatively simple. No need for a planner.
- To monitor a planner, you'll have to learn about investments anyway. So why get one?
- You do need financial advice from time to time. But you can get it without hiring a full-blown planner. You might be able to ask your friendly banker (if you actually have someone to talk to beyond your ATM) or read a book like this one.

Still, some people do need the help of a planner. But the word here is: Let the buyer (you) beware. Between 250,000 and 400,000 Americans call themselves financial planners and there are no federal or state regulations or licensing of this profession.

This combination of a complex subject and no government oversight makes the field as dangerous as a room

full of angry pit bull terriers. Here's what the cautious
consumer should do:

## 1. Check Credentials

Look for a planner who is certified by a major financial
planning organization. The best known are the Chartered
Financial Consultants (215-526-1000); the Institute of Certified Financial Planners (800-282-7526); the International
Association For Financial Planning (404-395-1605); and
the National Association of Personal Financial Advisors
(800-366-2732). Members of these groups have met educational requirements and have pledged to adhere to a
code of ethics. Call these groups for their ample
consumer-oriented planning literature. *Beware*: After you
call you will probably be contacted by at least one of the
group's members who practice in your area. If they get
too obnoxious call the NASD—National Association of
Securities Dealers (800-289-9999) to complain.

## 2. Ask Lots of Questions

Always interview potential planners. Ask them about
their education, experience, references, investment philosophy, and so on. What kind of clients does the planner
have? Can you see a sample plan they have prepared for
a client? Does the planner have a speciality?

## 3. Commission vs. Fee-Based

This is critical. Like brokers and insurance agents (many
of whom call themselves financial planners), most planners are paid by commission on the financial products

they sell. The $64,000 question is whether a planner who works on commission can give you objective financial advice? If you've found an honest planner, the answer is yes.

If you're not sure, look for a fee-only planner. (NAPFA members are all fee-only). Their fees, which may be hourly or fixed, can range from several hundred to several thousand dollars. What you'll get is a detailed written plan, which you can then choose to implement or not.

*Note:* In 1991, many brokers and mutual funds began to court smaller investors with planning services (the big investors have always had it). Shearson's TRAK Personalized Investment Advisory Service is one. For a minimum investment of $25,000, TRAK will advise you on allocating your money among ten different mutual funds. Price: 1.5% annually based on your assets under management.

(*Beware:* While TRAK will recommend investments from companies other than Shearson, some of these new services, like the ones offered by the Fidelity family of mutual funds, only recommend their own investments—not very objective).

## REAL-LIFE TIP

It was inevitable: Financial planners are putting on their headsets and dispensing advice on "900" telephone lines for $1 to $3 a minute. Marketing Logistics, a telecommunications consulting firm, predicts that this trend will grow over the next few years. (See chapter 8 for advice on using 900 numbers).

# Smart Investing

Back to basics: Don't put all your eggs in one basket. Divide up your dollars, schedule your transactions, and stick it out. And whether you're going to use a planner or not, you'll still need to know the rules of the game.

To buy a CD, you simply check local and out-of-town bank rates. You can open a money market account at a bank too, or shop for the types offered by mutual funds. Some bonds are also simple to buy.

Savings bonds can be purchased for as little as $25, and the federal government has a program called Treasury Direct which allows you to buy Treasury bonds yourself without paying any commission (call your regional Federal Reserve Bank for details or ask your bank for an application).

But what about stocks and other types of bonds? Traditionally, you would go to a stockbroker for advice on good investments and assistance in buying them, paying the broker a percentage of the purchase price. If you are savvy enough, and have the time to do your own research, you can use a discount broker, Charles Schwab or Quick & Reilly to name two. They'll place your orders for a much lower commission, often less than 1%.

If you decide to use a broker, ask your friends for recommendations. Then sit down with at least two and get a feel for their style. As a last check, contact your state's securities regulators (in your phone book) for any information they may have on this person and his or her company. If they don't have anything on record, try the North American Securities Administrators Association at 202-737-0900. Your state agency is your best bet though, so be sure to start your investigation there.

Buying individual stocks is fine for some of us. But for most small, novice investors there's a better way: mutual funds, more specifically no-load mutual funds.

A mutual fund is a pool of money contributed by many investors, large and small, which is invested and maintained by an expert "portfolio manager." Technically, investors do not own the stocks; they own shares in the collective fund.

Mutual funds have been around for a long time, but they really boomed after World War II. By the end of 1990, there were more than 3,000 funds with more than $1 trillion in assets invested by thirty million individuals and institutions. The funds come in all flavors. Some are diversified; some invest only in blue-chip companies; some in European firms; some in New York municipal bonds, and on and on. Some funds—multifunds—invest only in the shares of other funds! Here's why mutual funds are so popular:

1. IMPARTIAL EXPERTISE

Most of us don't have the time to study individual companies to see if they're good investments. We're too busy with our own careers and families to be expert financial analysts on the side. Stockbrokers can help, but since they're paid on commission their advice may be biased. With a mutual fund, you buy shares in a portfolio managed by an expert whose own pay hinges on the success of the fund.

2. EASY DIVERSIFICATION
Think of it: You have $5,000 to invest and you know you should diversify. If you bought individual stocks with your relatively small amount of money, you wouldn't be able to diversify beyond a few companies. With a mutual fund you get a share of the whole portfolio—which may consist of as many as one hundred companies.

---

## REAL-LIFE ISSUE:
## PROFITS VERSUS YOUR CONSCIENCE

"Maximize profits!" Some enlightened Boomers have decided to revise this cardinal rule of investing by launching the "socially responsible" investing movement in mutual funds. These funds, now with billions of dollars in assets, use varying social measures to guide their investments. Some avoid companies that do business in South Africa, some won't invest in firms having bad records on the treatment of unions or women. One, Working Assets, in San Francisco, at 1-800-533-3863, focuses on companies that are socially responsible and friendly to the environment.

---

## Take a Load Off: Cut Costs

So far, so good. But, like brokers, many mutual funds charge a sales commission—called a "load"—that can reach 8.5%. Avoid these "loaded" funds—often offered by the big brokerage houses. Studies show that, as a group, no-load and low-load funds do just as well as the loaded variety.

*Bottom Line:* No-load and low-load mutual funds are the best bet for most investors. To learn about them and use them wisely, follow these simple steps:

### 1. INVESTIGATE BEFORE YOU INVEST

Newspapers and magazines cover mutual funds regularly. Follow these reports for a while and you'll get the idea behind them. If possible, also read *The Handbook for No-Load Investors*, by Sheldon Jacobs. It's issued each year, and it's the best source on the subject. Also check out some of the sources that rate mutual funds (Morningstar and Lippert to name just two). You can subscribe to these companies' reports—a fairly hefty investment—but any decent library will probably carry at least one of these services.

### 2. COMPARE AND CONTRAST

Study the 3-year and 5-year performance records of mutual funds that interest you (these numbers can be found in the financial pages of most major newspapers). Pick a few top performers.

### 3. SEND FOR INFORMATION

Call a few of the funds, and read their prospectuses and other materials. If you have questions, call their toll-free numbers. They'll be happy to help you with your questions.

### 4. BEWARE OF THE FEES

No-loads don't charge sales commissions, but some no-loads and low-loads may impose redemption fees when you sell your shares, or annual marketing charges called 12b-1 fees—is nothing ever simple? There's another sneaky device called a "deferred contingent sales charge"—a delayed sales fee they hit you with if you sell your shares within a certain period of time.

Make sure that your fund doesn't charge these fees. Also make sure that the fund's "expense ratio"—its overall annual management costs—is no more than 1.5%. This number can be found in the fund's prospectus. (Remember that funds have minimum initial investments, usually between $1,000 and $3,000. These minimums may affect your choice.)

---

### REAL ADVISORY

In addition to mutual fund companies, banks, brokerage houses, insurance companies, pension groups, and discount brokers also sell mutual funds. They may jazz up the offer but the basics of buying the funds remain the same: Look for low costs and good performance.

---

So, you're an investor. You should always try to reinvest your dividends, and your gains, and buy more shares when you can (minimum investments are usually $100, sometimes $250). Track your fund, and the market in general, as best you can—this shouldn't take too much time.

## Scam Artists: Hold On To Your Wallet

Snake oil: There's plenty of it on Wall Street, and not all of its purveyors have pencil mustaches or work out of the back of horse-drawn carriages. Swindlers come in as many varieties as there are cereals in your local supermarket. Their only common trait is their intention to deceive you and relieve you of some of your hard-earned cash. And beware, they can be very skilled at their craft.

Consider the Infallible Forecaster Scam, one of the many scams used by your friendly neighborhood con artist. It goes something like this (*Note*: Use a Rod Serling voice as you read the next four paragraphs):

Maggie Miller, thirtysomething lawyer, gets a call from stockbroker Bill Carson (she didn't quite catch the name of his firm). Bill assures her that he doesn't want to sell her anything—a sure tip-off. He simply wants to clue her in to one of his firm's market forecasts ("Maggie is part of a select group to be contacted when the company makes its periodic predictions"). If, at some point in the future, Maggie is impressed with the firm's predictions, great. But Bill doesn't want to sell her anything right now.

Bill's first prediction: Land's End stock will soar within the next two weeks. Sure enough, it does. Maggie is impressed, but not ready to commit. Bill's second call comes about three weeks later, and again his next prediction comes true. When Bill's third forecast comes true, Maggie is frothing at the bit. She eagerly gives Bill her year-end bonus for him to invest.

Bye-bye bonus. Bye-bye Bill. Maggie fell hard for the Infallible Forecaster Scam. Bill's scam: He calls 100 people, tells 50 that the Land's End will rise and 50 that it will fall. When it rises, he takes the first 50 names and tells 25 of them that Stock $X$ will rise and 25 that it will fall. By the end of the third round, Bill has a dozen folks believing he's Nostradamus. Their checks are quickly written and sent to Bill at his post office box.

Investment scams often focus on oil and gas, gold, real estate, and penny stocks. They are usually targeted to "suckers" over the phone. If you have any doubts about a salesman's good faith, contact your local office of the Securities and Exchange Commission or other regulatory agency in your area.

Here are some other scam warning signs:

TOO GOOD—"IF IT'S TOO GOOD TO BE TRUE . . ."
If someone offers you a "can't-miss" investment with spectacular guaranteed profits, you should probably take a pass.

TOO FAST
When the salesperson says the deal can't wait until tomorrow, get suspicious and contact your local regulatory agency.

TOO MYSTERIOUS
Questions are a real turn-off for con artists. Ask lots of them. Ask for references, the names of his or her firm's principals, and prospectuses for the investment. Ask if he or she is willing to explain the offer to a third party—say, your accountant. If his or her answers are mumbled or you hear something like "Normally I would but time is of the essence," hang up and hold on to your checkbook.

TOO COMPLICATED
If the explanation of the investment sounds like a verbal Rubik's Cube, be cautious. Never invest in anything you don't understand.

# Paying For College

College: The word gives the shivers to all but the richest parents! Along with retirement, our children's education may be one of the most difficult financial hurdles we will face. And the news about total college costs—tuition, room and board, books and supplies, transportation, etc.—is not good. College costs easily outpaced inflation through most of the 1980s. The result is that if today's trends continue, a child born in 1990 will face a college bill of $100,000 for a state university (if they still exist in 2008), and $215,000 for a private college.

The rules of investing for college are similar to the rules of investing in general: Follow the four rules set out earlier and focus on no-load or low-load mutual funds. So, when your child is young, put the bulk of your kiddy's "kitty" into "growth-oriented" mutual funds. As the years go by, diversify some funds into bonds and CDs. As college approaches, gradually shift the funds into more conservative instruments.

## REAL-LIFE OPTION: PREPAY PROGRAMS

Terrified by tuition hikes? Florida, Michigan, Ohio, and some other states have something to calm your nerves— and you don't need a doctor's prescription to get it. You invest a certain amount now, or at regular intervals, and the state guarantees college tuition at one of its state schools when your child is ready to attend. The offer can ease your worries about inflation, but some experts say you're better off investing the money yourself and keeping your options open.

Another problem with these plans: What if your child decides that he or she wants to be a plumber (congratulations!), or an artist (my most sincere condolences), or simply wants to attend an out-of-state school? Make sure you can get your money back—with your earned interest—if you don't make use of the education.

Financing college tuition does have some special twists. For one, you have to begin saving early. Put away regular savings when little Tiffany is in diapers, and your monthly burden will be a few hundred dollars. But wait until she's in high school and your monthly tab may be a near-impossible $2,000.

Financial-aid rules also add some special considerations to your college planning. The main issue is the impact of "expected-contribution" standards on your choice of financing. Here are *today's* typical aid rules:

- Students may contribute up to 70% of their income and 35% of their assets toward their college costs each year.
- Parents must contribute up to 47% of their income and 5% to 6% of their assets (including equity in any homes or property) toward their children's college costs each year.

There's no need to be Phi Beta Kappa to figure this out. To shelter yourself from the storm of the expected-contribution rules, it's better to have assets instead of income and it's better to have funds in the parents' names instead of the student's. There are many clever ways to do these things, but for most people these rules guide us toward two important lessons:

## 1. Nix Those Gifts

The rules say that students must contribute a higher percentage toward college than their parents. This means that making outright gifts to children, or establishing a

custodial account in their name under the Uniform Gift to
Minors Act (UGMA), may be ill-advised. The goal of such
gifts is to take advantage of the usually lower child's tax
rate. Problem: The financial-aid disadvantage of such gifts
may be substantial. *Note*: The UGMA rules are complex,
and "gifting" may sometimes make sense. Ask your accountant or see *The MONEY College Guide* for more information. Another good source of publications on paying
for college is The College Board, a national not-for-profit
educational group (212-713-8000).

## 2. Save Anyway

You might be asking "Why save for college at all?" "The
more money we have the less aid we'll get." This reasoning may work for some, but for most of us it's unwise.
The required financial-aid contribution from parents is
only 5% to 6% each year—half the average annual return
on stocks. So, the payback to long-term investing is
greater than the price you'll pay in college contributions.
(Of course, if the aid rules change, it may become a different ballgame.)

Sharpen your pencils, and your wits. There are a few
more special considerations when thinking about college
costs. Here are the main ones:

### SERIES EE

Stocks should be your staple investment for college, but
new tax treatment for U.S. Savings Bonds of Series EE
makes them attractive. Always exempt from state and local taxes, EE bonds issued in 1990 or later are now also

exempt from federal tax—if the proceeds are used for college. CAUTION: This tax break has income restrictions. In 1990, for example, if your gross income was less than $40,000 (single) or $60,000 (married), you were eligible for a full exemption. The exemption is phased out for higher-income parents, however, disappearing completely for single parents with gross incomes of $55,000 or more and couples earning $90,000 or more—calculated when the bonds are cashed. These limits are adjusted for inflation from year to year.

ZEROES

Zero-coupon bonds pay no interest until they reach maturity. If you hold them until maturity, they can be appropriate college investments. A dozen states issue zeroes—sometimes called "baccalaureate bonds"—that are triple tax-free (federal, state, local). The U.S. Treasury sells zeroes too—but they're subject to federal taxes.

COLLEGE "DEALS"

Special "college investments," often found in CDs and insurance annuities, should be approached with as much caution as a sidewalk card game. Their college appeal is often just a ploy to cash in on your parental concerns. Judge them as you would any other investment.

LOANS

There are many government student loans that focus on lower-income families. But the best private source of low-

cost student loans and home equity loans (tax deductible), are from pensions and life insurance policies.

---

### REAL-LIFE DIALOGUE

CONFUSED PARENT: "I know that my wife and I should save
for college for our Tiffany, our twelve-year-old, but our
paychecks are gone before we know it. Any advice?"

REAL ANSWER: "Many mutual funds will automatically deduct a specific amount—as little as $25—from your
checking account each month. It's perfect for many of
us undisciplined savers."

---

## Gathering Nuts For Your Golden Years

Retirement calls for more than just bifocals and sensible
shoes. Like college, retirement is one of life's biggest financial hurdles. The three main issues are: How much
will you need? How much will you have? And—if there's
a gap—how can you best bridge it?

### 1. How Much You'll Need: (A lot!)

Insurers, banks, pension funds, financial how-to books:
They all have worksheets for calculating your appropriate
retirement income. But it's hard to plug in some of the
numbers they ask for—like how long you're going to live,
and the rate of inflation over the next fifty years.

The direction of these numbers may be easier to figure

than their specific values. Some factors will make your retirement needs lower: No job-related expenses like commuting and fancy clothes; a lower tax bracket; and less need for life insurance. In general, these items may make 70% of your preretirement income adequate for your senior years.

But for many of us Baby Boomers, certain things point toward a larger need in our later years:

- We'll live longer than previous generations.
- We may have to shell out larger sums for health insurance.
- Unlike our parents, many of us are having children later—we may be paying our children's tuition close to or even during our retirement years.
- We can't expect the sustained rise in real estate values that our parents enjoyed during the postwar years.

What do all of these trends mean? To make it real, here's some typical number-crunching: A 35-year-old earning $50,000 and hoping to retire at age 60 will need $120,000 a year during retirement, adjusted for inflation. GULP!

## 2. What You've Got:
## (Probably less than you think)

How much of that $120,000—or $100,000 or $150,000—will be taken care of by Social Security and your pension (if you have one)? To find out—and it's crucial to do so—take these steps now:

- *Call* the Social Security Administration at 800-772-1213 and ask for Form 7004, "Request for Personal Earnings and Benefit Estimate Statement." Make sure that the SSA record of your earnings is right (there are estimated to be as many as 11 million Social Security records containing mistakes), and then fill out the form. In about a month, you'll get an estimate of your retirement benefits.

- *Ask* your pension officer at work for a similar estimate. The chances are that these numbers—which are only a crude measure—will be far less than your estimated retirement needs. For Baby Boomers, the news will probably get even worse. Here's why:

SOCIAL (IN)SECURITY

Social Security is wonderful. It covers most U.S. workers (you must work at least forty quarters to qualify), and it's benefits have COLAs—cost-of-living adjustments—that protect you from the effects of inflation. But, for many of us, Social Security will probably get weaker as we get closer to our retirement. In the year 2020, for example, it's projected that benefits, in real dollars, will be 22% less than they are now, and the current eligibility age of 65 is scheduled to become 66 in 2005 and 67 in 2022.

PENSIONS

Like Social Security, pensions are wonderful. They cover 50% of the private U.S. workforce and 75% of government employees, but they often have strict limits. Seventy-five percent have no COLAs, and some are "pegged" to Social Security, so that the more you get of one the less you get of the other. Also troubling is the precarious state of many pension funds: The nation's fifty largest under-funded pension plans—covering 40 million workers—had a combined shortfall of $21.5 billion in late 1991. YIKES!

---

### REAL-LIFE TIP

Vesting: No, it's not something a tailor does. It's the period of time—typically five to seven years—during which workers acquire the right to their pensions. *Good Idea*: If you're contemplating a job switch, check the vesting rules of your current employer. You may have only a month to go before you get vested.

---

## 3. Self-Reliance in the Sunset Years

The lesson here for later life: Social Security and your pension may pay for your hammock and your subscription to *Modern Maturity*, but you'll have to find some other sources of income too.

Luckily, there are several tax-advantaged investments to consider. Their two main tax benefits—tax deduction and tax deferral—will let your money grow much faster than a taxable investment. Added bonus (sort of): In most cases, the IRS will levy a 10% penalty if you withdraw money from these accounts before you turn 59½. For those of us without self-discipline, think of it as a forced savings plan! You can't touch the money without facing a substantial penalty.

*Best Advice:* Use these tax-advantaged strategies to the max; you may be able to avoid using taxable investments entirely as you prepare for retirement. And—as always— follow our four basic rules of investing.

### A. IRAs

No, not the guys who want England out of Ireland: Individual Retirement Accounts. Everyone under age 70½ who receives earned income can contribute up to $2,000 each year to an IRA. Moreover, IRA earnings are tax-deferred until they are paid out during your retirement. The tax deferral alone makes IRAs worth it. But for some people, all or part of their contribution of up to $2,000 is also tax-deductible.

Regardless of income, for example, a person without a pension plan can deduct his or her IRA contribution in full. The IRA contribution is also completely deductible for persons with adjusted gross incomes of less than $25,000 (single) or $40,000 (married). And there is a partial phased-out deduction for those having pensions whose adjusted gross incomes are between $25,000 and $35,000 (single) and between $40,000 and $50,000 (married).

Whether the contribution is fully or partly deductible, or even not deductible at all, the tax-deferral advantage of IRAs is too good to ignore.

## GET REAL!

In 1990, 67 million workers were eligible to contribute to a fully deductible IRA. Amazingly, only 15% actually did so.

### B. SECTION 401(K) PLANS

Run by some employers, section 401(k) plans (named for the Internal Revenue Code section pursuant to which they are established) are "voluntary salary-reduction agreements," sometimes called "Super IRAs" because the maximum contribution is more than four times the IRA limit. Twenty-five percent of full-time U.S. workers are eligible for 401(k)'s. Like IRAs, 401(k) earnings grow tax-deferred, but unlike IRAs, the contribution is always tax-deductible.

Some employers even sweeten the pot by matching or contributing some percentage of the employee's 401(k) contributions. But you may have to stay with your company for a certain number of years before you are entitled to get the company's contribution. Government and not-for-profit employees have their own version of the 401(k)—the 403(b).

### C. KEOGHS

Named for the congressman who invented them, Keoghs are "Super IRAs" for the self-employed. They are also known as H.R. 10 plans. Like 401(k)'s and 403(b)'s, they also carry the important tax benefits of deductibility and deferral. The maximum contribution, which can be as much as $30,000 each year, depends on your net self-employment income and the kind of Keogh plan you set up.

*Note:* Even if you are a full-time employee, you can set up a Keogh if you have any self-employment income. Smart idea: Start a home-based business that allows you to continue with your full-time job. There are requirements that must be met, but you'll be able to enjoy the benefits of a Keogh plan AND deduct a portion of many of your home's costs (heat, electricity, rent or mortgage, etc.).

## INVESTOR ADVISORY

While many investments are "self-managed"—handled by the investor—many retirement accounts, with the exception of IRAs, are managed by big pension funds or insurers. You should monitor these "other-managed" accounts for their adherence to our four rules of investing. Are their investments appropriate? Are their expenses too high? If you're not happy with the answers to your questions, you can withdraw your funds and manage them yourself—as you do with your IRA. It all boils down to a single principle of retirement: self-reliance.

# Getting the Most for Your Money

You like to spend money and everyone wants your hard-earned cash. But how do you protect yourself against deceptive marketing tactics and clever scam artists? The best thing you can do is to become aware of the tricks of the trade and arm yourself against inevitable assaults from the REAL world. Here are some tips:

## How Do You Pay

### 1. Cash
Still accepted at SOME locations, cash is still the preferred form of payment, particularly for our parents' generation.

PROS:
- Feels good in your pocket.
- Still universally accepted at retail outlets in the United States.

CONS:

- Wears out.
- Gets your hands dirty.
- Carries germs.
- Can't carry any personalized messages (legally).
- Doesn't provide a built-in record of transactions.
- Not accepted for telephone ordering.
- Not accepted at many international locations.
- Easily lost or stolen.

---

## SHOPPER'S TIP

If you're paying with cash (or a check, which is basically a cash equivalent since retailers pay no service charge), ask the store manager for a cash discount. Remember, he or she is saving the credit card fee—usually 3% or more—and should be willing to at least split the difference with you. Don't be afraid to haggle—it's your money.

---

## 2. Checks

PROS:

- Safer than cash.
- Can carry your personalized or decorative message ("Save the Whales," "Elvis Lives," "Nuke the Whales").
- Provides a record of transactions.

CONS:

- Inconvenient to use.
- Often requires additional identification.
- Not accepted for telephone transactions.
- Not accepted at certain locations.

Checks are fairly safe to carry. If they're stolen, you're generally free from liability for any fraudulent usage. You can also stop payment on a check in the event you:

- Don't get what you paid for.
- Receive damaged goods.
- Were deceived by the salesperson.

Some states even allow you to change your mind regarding a check purchase, so long as you do so within a few days. Call your local consumer protection agency regarding your state's so-called "cooling off" regulations.

If you decide to stop payment on a check, make sure you:

DO IT QUICKLY

Merchants often race to their bank with checks to get faster payment. If your check gets processed before you stop payment, you're out of luck.

PROVIDE YOUR BANK WITH AN EXPLANATION

You'll probably call your bank, so make sure to get a confirmation from them in writing that includes your reason for the action.

RETURN THE MERCHANDISE AS SOON AS POSSIBLE

In the case of a service (health club membership, dating service contract, etc.), notify the company of your change of heart and your reason for stopping the transaction. If you're returning goods that were purchased by mail, get a return receipt that will prove that the goods were actually returned.

*Note:* You'll probably have to pay a small fee to your bank to stop payment on a check (usually $5 to $10).

---

### REAL CAUTION

Many retailers ask for two forms of identification when you pay with a check, usually a driver's license and a major credit card. PROBLEM: Anyone having your name, address, phone number, and credit card information can easily order merchandise over the phone using this information and have the goods shipped to another address—their own.

---

Another scam can occur when someone steals your personal information (including your Social Security number, which appears on many state's driver's licenses) and applies for new credit in your name. The thief can then run up huge bills on "your account" and quickly put your credit record into intensive care.

*How do you protect yourself?* At least one state (Iowa) now prohibits retailers from asking for your credit card number when you write a check. If you're not currently

living in the Hawkeye state, you can still refuse to give
your credit card number when paying with a check.
Stores are still allowed by law to refuse your purchase,
but in these economic times what are the chances of
that happening? If they do protest, tell them what you
know about this kind of fraud and alert them to these
facts:

1. Most credit card companies won't cover a bad
   check anyway.
2. Even without your credit card information, they
   have enough information to find you if your check
   bounces.
3. They can now subscribe to at least one check autho-
   rizing service which will guarantee customer
   checks for a small fee. TeleCheck, which acts like a
   credit card authorization service, is just one such
   service now in operation.

## 3. Credit Cards
Fun! ... And you don't even have to pay until, well ...
whenever.

PROS:
- Safer than cash.
- Easy to use.
- Can carry logo of an idealogically appropriate group
  (affinity cards).
- Accepted internationally.
- Accepted for telephone transactions.
- Provide free grace (float) period.

- Provide deferred payment option.
- Provide record of transactions.

CON:
- Dangerous for those with less-than-military discipline.

If your credit card is stolen, you're free from any liability for any fraudulent usage, provided you report the card as stolen before anyone uses it. If the card is used before you contact your credit card company you're only responsible for the first $50 of charges. If your card is not physically stolen but your number is used without your knowledge, you have no liability.

If you purchase damaged or defective goods with a credit card, notify your credit card issuer within sixty days of the purchase with the news that you're not going to pay. *Note*: You can only withhold the portion of your bill that's in dispute and, if you've already paid for part of the purchase, you can only withhold the remaining balance.

What you are doing is holding the credit card company responsible for the problem. They will either try to get payment from the merchant or try to get it from you. In the latter case, you could get into a dispute with the credit card company and eventually earn a black mark on your credit record. It's always better to try to resolve your dispute with the merchant as soon as possible. If they won't cooperate, then repeat that you're not going to pay.

## REAL CAUTION (Part II)

When paying with a credit card, many sales clerks will ask for your home address and phone number. DON'T COMPLY! This information can be used to put you on a mailing list or, worse, enable a bad guy to charge goods and services to your account. Remember, even a request for your telephone number is an invasion of privacy.

Remind the store owner that he or she is fully protected as long as they get your signature and an authorization number from the credit card company. If you don't pay, it's the credit card company, and not you, who is liable. Unlike checks, a merchant cannot refuse your purchase if you withhold your address or phone number during a credit card transaction. Certain states and Visa, MasterCard, and American Express prohibit retailers from refusing a sale for this reason. If the store hassles you, and you really want that new CD player, simply put down a phony address and phone number.

FOR FURTHER PROTECTION:
1. Draw a line through any unused spaces on the charge receipt.
2. Save your charge receipts and compare them with your billing statements. If you find an error, complain within sixty days.
3. Destroy your carbons and old credit slips.

## 4. Debit Cards

PROS:
- Safer than cash.
- Convenient to use.
- Accepted at a growing number of locations.
- Provide record of transactions.

CONS:
- No grace period.
- No deferred payment option.

As long as you report your debit card as stolen within a few days (generally two to four), you're liable for only the first $50 of any fraudulent usage. The longer you wait, however, whether you are aware of the theft or not, the greater your liability. Read your monthly statements and compare the company's records with your own.

If you purchase defective or damaged goods, your protection will largely depend upon the company that issued your card. There are no general industry standards on this issue yet. Check the company's policies before signing up.

# Financing

Whether you pay "cash," or choose to finance a purchase, depends on a number of issues:
- The item being purchased (how long will it last and whether it is likely to lose or gain value?)

- The cost (can I easily pay for it with available cash?)
- The terms (interest rate, length of loan, fees, etc.) being offered
- The tax-deductibility of the interest
- Your own personal situation (are you already carrying too much debt?)

While you'll usually benefit by paying cash, the issue is not as clear-cut as you might think.

EXAMPLE 1: Let's say you buy a new car for $10,000—a small car! If you borrow the $10,000 from a bank at, say, 8½% over four years, you'll pay about $1,800 in nondeductible interest. If you pay for the car with cash from your savings instead, you'll lose approximately $1,100 in after-tax interest income (assuming a 4% return and a 30% combined federal and state tax obligation). Your advantage of paying cash under this scenario is about $700. If you borrow the money for the purchase using a home equity loan, where the interest is tax-deductible, the benefit of paying cash would be smaller.

## REAL CAUTION

If you decide to use cash from savings to make a purchase, you'll have to be very disciplined if your goal is to replace the money you've taken from the account. Miss just a couple of monthly payments to yourself (using the money you would have otherwise paid to the bank each month), and you'd have been better off borrowing.

EXAMPLE 2: Borrowing may make sense if you can get the money at a lower interest rate than you might enjoy on your after-tax investments. This is a relatively unusual scenario that may develop through manufacturers' or dealers' incentive programs (car makers and their dealers often sponsor low-interest-rate loans to move excess inventory). WARNING: Be careful that your super low interest rate isn't being offset by higher prices or hidden extras on the car.

You should never use up all of your savings to make a purchase. As a general rule of thumb, you should always keep enough cash (including so-called "liquid investments" that can be sold quickly without significant penalties or loss of equity) on hand to cover at least six months worth of expenses—twelve months is probably a better idea in these "nutty '90s."

If you decide to buy with borrowed money, be sure to consider the following principles.

SHOP AROUND FOR THE BEST DEAL ON A LOAN
There can be large differences in the rates offered by retail stores, banks, credit unions, etc. Don't automatically accept the store's credit plan because it's easier than shopping around.

CONSIDER USING A HOME EQUITY LOAN to finance your purchase. Getting the money out of your home makes the loan tax-deductible. *Caveat*: You're putting your home on the line to buy a car, clothes dryer, wide-screen TV, or other depreciating asset. You'll also end up paying more interest on the loan since the term of your home loan will probably be longer than any consumer loan.

CONSIDER BORROWING AGAINST YOUR LIFE INSURANCE POLICY
If you have a cash value (whole life) policy, you can borrow against your principal at favorable interest rates. Problem: The interest you pay is not tax-deductible.

CONSIDER BORROWING FROM A FAMILY MEMBER
Both parties can benefit from this type of arrangement, assuming you make your loan payments on time. Your lender gets an above-market rate on his or her investment and you get a below-market rate on your loan, with no closing costs.

# Getting What You Paid For

There's no shame in getting what you pay for. The status symbols of the 1980s are being quickly replaced by a new emphasis on value and durability. While a BMW may have inspired looks of longing and appreciation just a few short years ago, most luxury items are now greeted with comments concerning wastefulness, greed, and twisted priorities. While some of this reaction is undoubtedly brought on by jealousy (who wouldn't want that new sports car), the times are certainly changing.

# How to Be a Sophisticated Shopper

Getting what you paid for requires constant vigilance. Learn the tricks of the trade and know your rights. Begin this process by following these steps:

## 1. Get to Know the Companies You're Dealing With

Check out their reputations by contacting your state or local department of consumer affairs and your local chapter of the Better Business Bureau. They'll give you an idea of the organization's business practices. ADVICE: Don't deal with shifty companies. It's not worth any initial savings you might realize. If the particular industry has a state or local licensing board, make sure that the company you plan to deal with has a current and valid license.

Also, as you're beginning your search, ask your friends and neighbors for recommendations and references. Spending a little time in advance can save you a great deal of time, money, and heartache in the long run.

## 2. Understand What You're Getting Into

This may mean carefully reading a service contract BEFORE you sign it, or learning a store's return or delivery policy BEFORE you make a purchase. There's no substitute for good preparation. *Remember:* Don't be afraid to ask "stupid questions."

## 3. Look at the Warranties
## Before You Make a Purchase

Before you decide to buy a certain item at a particular
store, be sure to consider more than just style and price.
Make sure you also check the store's and the manufacturer's warranties. A common example of consumer confusion in this area involves the sale of "gray market"
electronics. Certain stores may get products that were intended for sale in other countries. The products don't
carry the usual manufacturers' warranty because they
may have been rebuilt, damaged in transit, or built to
lower standards for sale in a less restrictive market. In
this case you will have only the retail store to hold responsible if the product fails. Good Luck trying to get satisfaction on a return from a store called "Krazeeee Kurt's
Discount Bizarre."

WHAT CAN YOU DO TO PROTECT YOURSELF?

*Deal Only With Reputable Companies.* It's worth the few
extra dollars and cents.

*Read the Warranties Before You Buy.* You may feel a little
foolish, and pressured, while you read through these materials, but so what! If the store is hesitant to give you
copies of the warranties, politely refer them to the
Magnuson-Moss Act of 1975, which requires that all warranties be available for consumers to read before they
make a purchase. Be sure to consider these questions as
you're reading:

- What problems are covered?
- What expenses are covered? Some warranties cover the cost of parts, but not the labor required to install them.
- How long does the coverage last?
- Are there any conditions on the warranty? For example, is the warranty on your new computer voided if you use low-grade floppy discs?
- Who provides the service?
- Will the warranty cover any personal losses caused by a malfunction (food spoiled by a broken freezer, work lost because of a down computer, etc.).

*Get the Warranty in Writing.* Don't accept a salesperson's promises without also getting them to put it in writing.

*Keep the Sales Receipt and Your Warranty in a Safe Place.* You'll probably need to present both of these documents if you have a problem.

## 4. Beware of Service Contracts

Sold as "peace of mind," service contracts are most popular among buyers of new cars—although used-car and major appliance purchasers often buy them as well. These contracts can indeed give you peace of mind but you may be paying for something that you already have or don't really need. Before you lay down good money on a service contract, be sure to ponder the following questions:

A. HOW MUCH DOES IT COST?
Unlike warranties, which are included free with the purchase, service contracts must be purchased separately.

B. WHO IS PROVIDING THE CONTRACT?
It may be a small company with shaky finances located in rural Ohio. Only deal with stable businesses that have insurance—check them out with your consumer agencies.

C. WHAT DOES THE CONTRACT COVER?
See how much of this protection is already included in your product's free warranty.

D. WHAT COSTS DOES IT COVER?
There may be a deductible for each service episode.

E. HOW LONG DOES THE COVERAGE LAST?
A contract that lasts beyond your warranty term may make sense. See if you can purchase the contract after your warranty expires.

F. WHO PERFORMS THE SERVICE?
Is the work done at the store or do you have to deal with a regional service firm or, worse, send the item to a repair facility in Oshkosh, Wisconsin?

G. CAN THE CONTRACT BE TRANSFERRED TO A NEW OWNER?
This is particularly important in the case of new or used cars.

## 5. Avoid Layaway Plans

I always thought that layaway plans provided the same basic service as buying on store-provided credit. WRONG! When using a layaway plan, and I strongly suggest that you do not, you pay for your purchase in installments BEFORE you actually take delivery of the item.

What is the problem here? First, the store has your money and you have no merchandise. Second, there are no federal regulations regarding the conduct of these plans. You may have no place to turn if you have a problem. Check with your state or local agencies regarding any local laws that cover these plans. If you insist on getting involved, be sure to follow these instructions:

A. Check out the store's reputation by contacting your local consumer agencies.

B. Understand the terms of any deal you are considering BEFORE you sign anything.

C. Find out what the interest rate is, what the payment period is, and whether there are any extra service fees.

D. Are there any penalties for late payments. You could be charged a fee, or even lose your merchandise, if you're even a couple of days late with a single payment.

E. Learn the store's refund policy. You should be able to cancel your purchase at any time, right?—Ha! Make sure that you can change your mind, and what the penalties are if you do.

F. Make sure your merchandise is set aside for you pending the completion of your payments. Suppose you finally finish paying for that 1950s style loveseat and it's suddenly out of stock.

## 6. Don't Be Afraid to Use Coupons

Does this sound familiar? "I will never clip coupons, do you hear me? Never!" There's nothing to be ashamed of here! Coupons are OK. Just make sure you use them only to purchase items that you would have bought anyway. The only danger in coupons is the urge we might get to buy "Fruity Choco-Loops" cereal for our kids because we find a $1-off coupon in our local newspaper.

Take the time to look through the coupons and try to find stores that offer double, or even triple redemption days. As with most things, this will take some time. You have to weigh the reward (money saved) against the loss of time.

## 7. Watch Out for Some Famous Scams

There are two common marketing schemes that you may have the pleasure of confronting at a retail store near you: "Bait-and-Switch" and "Loss Leaders."

In a "Bait-and-Switch" scam, you typically enter a store holding an advertisement for a particular item at a tantalizingly low price. The salesperson apologetically informs you that the product you want is sold out. He then directs your attention to another "very similar item" that is "actually much better," and just "slightly more expensive" than the one you THOUGHT you wanted. WATCH OUT! I know you drove a long way to get to this store, but so does your salesperson. Ask for a raincheck on the advertised item. *Note:* Unless the ad states that the item is available in limited quantities, the store is required to have enough on hand to satisfy "reasonable demand." A raincheck is not enough to cover them legally but few consumers go to the trouble of reporting a company for this deceptive business practice.

"Loss Leaders" entice you to enter a particular store with a very low advertised price on a commonly used item—diapers or milk, for example. It is the store's calculated hope that once you enter its premises to buy the diapers, you will also grab some regular and premium-priced items as well. After all, how many people can buy just one thing at *any* store?

## Shopping By Mail-Order

It's fun! It's easy! It's a toll-free number! You don't have to pay any sales tax (if you order from an out-of-state company—at least for the time being) and you don't even have to leave your LA-Z-BOY to do it. So it shouldn't be a surprise to anyone that more Americans are choosing to shop by mail.

While the number of mail-order complaints has been surprisingly low, it's still a good idea to know how to deal with mail-order companies and protect your rights if something goes wrong.

# 1. Basic Rules

### A. ALWAYS CHECK OUT THE COMPANY

Contact the Direct Marketing Association (they'll probably only tell you if the company is a member in good standing), your state or local department of consumer affairs, or the Better Business Bureau to get some information.

### B. MAKE SURE YOU CAN RETURN
### THE MERCHANDISE FOR ANY REASON

You don't have the luxury of holding that fishing rod in your hand or trying on that faux diamond ring before you order.

### C. KEEP A COPY OF YOUR ORDER FORM AND
### THE COMPANY INFORMATION

This will make it easier to track the merchandise if you have a problem.

### D. NEVER SEND CASH THROUGH THE MAIL

Checks and credit cards give you added safety from theft and offer some recourse in the event you end up in a dispute with the company.

### E. INSPECT THE MERCHANDISE
### AS SOON AS YOU RECEIVE IT

If there's a problem, e.g., it's defective in some way or you didn't order a solar-powered pith helmet, look for the company's return procedures in the catalog or shipping invoice. If you can't find any, or it's unclear in any way, call the company as soon as possible. If you receive goods by mistake, the company is responsible for the return postage.

## 2. What Are Your Rights?

Unless another time period is specified at the time of the purchase, the seller is required to ship your goods within thirty days from the time it receives your order. If it cannot meet this deadline for whatever reason, it's required to give you the option to cancel the purchase. Beware: If you don't respond to this option, usually sent on a postcard, you automatically give the seller the right to establish a new shipping deadline. If you ask to cancel the purchase, the seller must refund your money within seven business days. *Note*: For some unknown reason, these rules don't yet apply to orders that are placed via 800 numbers and charged to a credit card. In this case you can turn to your credit card company for protection.

## 3. What Can I Do If I Have a Problem?

You should always try to resolve your problems with the merchant. If you can't get any satisfaction from the mail-order company, you have many places to turn. Contact at least one of the following organizations:

A. The Direct Marketing Association's Mail-Order Action Line, 212-768-7277. They will contact the company and try to get the problem resolved. You will be asked to send in a letter stating the nature of your complaint and including any back-up materials you might have such as copies of the order, invoice, etc.

B. Your local or state department of consumer affairs.

C. Your state attorney general's office.

D. Your local Better Business Bureau.

E. The U.S. Postal Service's inspection service. Ask at your local post office for more information.

F. The Federal Trade Commission, 6th Street & Pennsylvania Avenues, N.W., Washington, D.C. 20580.

Remember to always complain in writing and be sure to document your problem and any steps you have taken to date.

# Protecting Yourself and Your Money

## "Because Nobody's Going To Do It For You"

---

## Junk Mail

If you're like most people, you probably imagine that an ancient redwood tree must be consumed just to produce the junk mail that terrorizes your mailbox each day. In reality, about one and one-half mature trees are used to produce your share of junk mail each year. Multiply that by 250 million Americans and you have, well, a lot of trees. What's worse, only 10% of that junk mail is ever recycled.

You might ask: "Why do they send me all this stuff?" In business-reality logic the answer is that it's an effort to bypass the major advertising media and get your attention in a more "direct" way. They're actually happy if just a few people out of every hundred people who receive their offering actually buy something.

"But a catalog just for fishing hooks?"

As you probably know, there are now catalogs for specialty decaffeinated coffees, pink Florida grapefruits, gay X-rated videos, and, yes, even those "wonderful" holiday fruitcakes (yech!). You name it, and eventually a catalog for it will find its way into your mailbox—not to mention the charitable solicitations, coupons for free chimney cleaning appraisals, and offers for free credit cards.

## REAL HERO

The hero in this real-life story is none other than your friendly neighborhood mail carrier. Not only does he or she have to put up with vicious dogs, angry customers, and the wind and the rain and the dark of night, but he or she also has to contend with pounds and pounds of junk mail.

To be sure, there may be some real social benefits to junkmail. For one, junk mail can make you feel alive—there's nothing worse than peering into an empty mailbox. Just ask Charlie Brown. And let's not forget:

*"You May Have Already Won $1,000,000*
*From the Publishers Clearinghouse."*

## 1. Is There Such a Thing as Good Junk Mail?

Some good things can show up in your 3rd class mail (the preferred vehicle for direct marketers). There are some very good direct mail companies in business today, and they do provide a real service. Since both husband and wife work in 59% of today's married-couple households, time to shop is limited and more and more people are shopping by mail. In addition to being a timesaver, shopping by mail gives you the unique opportunity to shop from the comfort and convenience of your living room. Also, you may be able to purchase items that aren't available in any nearby stores. And for the time being at least, you'll avoid paying any sales tax—provided you order from an out-of-state company that doesn't operate a retail store or warehouse in your state.

## 2. Dealing With Junk Mail Overload

While you may find some of it useful, the volume of junk mail reaching your home may become too much for even the loneliest of individuals to bear. What can you do if this is the case? For one thing, you can contact the industry's main trade group, the Direct Marketing Association, and ask that your name be taken off their members' lists.

*Write* to: Mail Preference Service c/o Direct Marketing Association, P.O. Box 9008, Farmingdale, NY 11735-9008. This should eliminate anywhere from two-thirds to three-quarters of your problem. *Note*: You'll have to provide the DMA with all of the possible spellings of your name. So, for example, if Elvis Presley—whatever his current mailing address might be—wanted to cut down on the arrival of junkmail to his mailbox, he would probably have to provide the DMA with the following variations of his name: Elvis Presley, E. Presley, and possibly even "The King." Check your junk mail for any misspellings of your name and include these on your request. Allow at least six weeks for your request to be processed.

## REAL TIP

If you order from direct mail companies after you ask to be taken off the DMA's lists, you will almost certainly start receiving some of the same annoying junk mail again. Almost all direct marketers earn extra money by renting their customers' names and addresses through list rental companies.

You can also contact companies directly, via their 800 numbers, and ask that your name be taken off their rental list. Direct mail companies are now required by law to make consumers aware of their intention to rent your name to other marketers. They are obligated to provide you with information on how you can ask them to keep your name off this file and out of the hands of other marketers.

## Telemarketing

In what might be more appropriately called "Junkphone," telemarketing has become a real test of our patience and understanding. At times, I feel like I'm in a low-budget horror film, running from the "Evil Marketers" who have just landed on Earth. This real-life battle between the marketers' right to free speech and your right to privacy is taking place on a strangely familiar battlefield—your telephone.

## REAL QUESTION

Which of these calls would you rather receive during dinner tonight:

1. Your mother-in-law calling to discuss your career
   prospects, or lack thereof.
2. Your boss calling to discuss that big deal you just blew.
3. An automated dialing machine calling to congratu-
   late you on the free trip to Disneyworld you've just
   won—if you just call 900-UB-STUPID within the
   next thirty minutes.

As you probably already know—unless you've been living in a cave or a biosphere—the country's marketers are
coming up with new ways to assault our privacy. They're
coming in through our televisions, radios, mail, telephones,
and even our fax machines. What's next? A sponsor-
emblazened Santa Claus climbing down our chimneys?

## REAL-LIFE NIGHTMARE

True story: An automated dialing machine enters a suburban hospital's main switchboard. After giving its robotic
message to the very frustrated switchboard operator, it
proceeds to dial every number in the hospital—including
nurses' stations, patient recovery rooms, and even operating suites.

While new laws have placed restrictions on the use of
autodialers and the sending of "junkfaxes," it's becoming

increasingly clear—to me anyway—that telemarketers have crossed that line in the sand. They must be stopped! It's time to stop being so damn nice to those annoying people and machines who/that always seem to call during dinner or that special romantic moment. Here is something you can do to "take back your phone" from these marketing maniacs.

Contact the industry's main trade group, the Direct Marketing Association, and ask that your name be taken off their telemarketing lists.

Write to: Telephone Preference Service, c/o Direct Marketing Association, P.O. Box 9014, Farmingdale, New York, NY 11735-9014. Provide all of the possible spellings of your name and all of your phone numbers, if you have more than one. Allow about six weeks for your request to be processed.

SIX TIP-OFFS THAT YOU'VE BEEN
CALLED BY A TELEMARKETER
1. "Hello, we're conducting a survey . . ."
2. "Hello, you've won a free gift."
3. "Congratulations on the birth of your new baby!"
4. "Congratulations on the purchase of your new home!"
5. "Is T. Smith at home?"
6. "Is the person who does your grocery shopping at home?"

*Or:*
7. They mispronounce your name.
8. They sound like a robot—they probably are.

HOW TO RESPOND TO A TELEMARKETER

1. Put your toddler on the line.
2. Try to sell THEM something.
3. Say that you don't accept phone solicitations and politely hang up.
4. Tell them that you just lost your job (they'll probably hang up on you).
5. Announce that you have Call-Trace and you're going to report their number to the police.

QUESTION: IS THERE EVER ANY GOOD REASON TO TALK TO A TELEMARKETER?
Yes ........................................... If you're feeling *very* lonely.

*Or:* If you really do want to have your chimney cleaned by a firm that, by some strange coincidence, is going to be in your exact neighborhood next week.

---

# Telefraud

---

If you do decide to talk to a telemarketer, be certain to ask yourself the following questions:

- Are you feeling pressured to make a decision?
- Does their offer sound too good to be true?
- Do they refuse to send you any free information that explains their offer?
- Are they unwilling to have you call them back?

- Are they asking you for a credit card number?
- Are they asking you to pay for a "FREE" prize?

If you answered yes to any of these questions, or feel uneasy for any reason at all, hang up.

1. SELF-DEFENSE

Follow these steps and you too can become a black-belt in telemarketing self-defense, a Bruce Lee, if you will, of consumer protection:

A. *DON'T* get pushed into making a decision. You should always be able to take advantage of that "great deal" tomorrow.

B. *ALWAYS* ask for something in writing before doing business with an unknown caller.

C. *NEVER* give out your credit card number over the phone, unless you are purchasing goods or services from a legitimate business.

D. *ALWAYS* ask for references.

E. *ALWAYS* check out the company with your local consumer organization or Better Business Bureau.

2. 900 NUMBERS

If you insist on calling a 900 number, you probably deserve any trouble you get. On the other hand, who am I to talk. We're all human and on more than one occassion, I too have been tempted to call 1-900-MADONNA.

*Beware:* 900 number services can charge whatever they want. There also aren't any guidelines regarding the quality or age-appropriateness of their messages. Read the fine print (if you can see it) and be prepared to complain. Do not call a 900 number until you know what it costs.

> **REAL SOLUTION**
>
> On your request, local telephone companies will now block any "900" numbers from being dialed from your home or business.

3. PROBLEMS

If you have a problem with phone fraud, contact these agencies for help (but remember, most victims of phone fraud don't get their money back—prevention is your best cure):

- Your local telephone company.
- Your local department of consumer affairs.
- Your state attorney general's office.
- The Federal Communications Commission, Enforcement Division, 1919 M Street, N.W., Washington, D.C. 20554.
- The Federal Trade Commission, Division of Marketing Practices, 6th Street and Pennsylvania Avenue, N.W., Washington, D.C. 20580.

# Charities

In the classic tale of Robin Hood, this popular kind hearted outlaw asked the people of Nottingham to provide him with alms for the poor. And as they were able, the Nottinghamians responded generously. Today, if Robin Hood were to approach any of our homes looking for contributions, we would probably do one of the following:

- Call the cops. After all, he is a guy in a green costume carrying a bow and arrow.
- Make believe we weren't home.
- Tell him to "get a job!"

At the very least, we would probably view Robin Hood with some very serious skepticism. After all, he doesn't have a permanent address (other than Sherwood Forest), he doesn't have a letterhead for his organization, and he isn't recognized by any government agency. It would also be hard to find out what percentage of his proceeds go toward overhead (the feeding of Little John and the Merry Men, for example), and how much of the money actually goes to the needy, things you should consider when deciding how much to give, and to whom.

Without a doubt, it is nobler to give than to receive. But who should you give to, and who can you trust? These questions, among others, can turn what should be a relatively simple act of generosity into a very stressful undertaking.

## 1. How Do You Protect Yourself When Giving to a Charity?

A. CHECK OUT THE ORGANIZATION YOU PLAN TO HELP. You can contact any of the following organizations for assistance:

- The Better Business Bureau's Philanthropic Advisory Service, 4200 Wilson Blvd., Arlington, VA 22203-1804, 703-276-0100.
- The National Charities Information Bureau, 19 Union Square West, Dept FT, New York, NY 10003-3395, 212-929-6300.
- The Internal Revenue Service. Publication 78 compiled by the IRS lists charities to which tax-deductible contributions can be made. To inquire about a particular organization, you should call 800-829-1040 and expect a reply by mail within seven to ten days. You could also check in your local public library to see whether they have a copy of this book. You might also want to ask the organization to show you a copy of their tax-determination letter which is provided by the IRS to all not-for-profit organizations.
- Your state attorney general's office. Many states monitor and sometimes even regulate the charities doing business within the state.
- Your local Better Business Bureau office. Only applicable in the case of regional charities.

B. MAKE SURE THE CHARITY GIVES MOST OF ITS LOOT TO THE ACTUAL CAUSES. Generally speaking, you should look for groups that put at least 70% of their income toward programs. Some do even better, but many spend too much on salaries, plush offices, and expensive fundraising efforts. To find out how a group will spend YOUR money, ask for an annual report.

C. BE WARY OF TELEPHONE APPEALS. Always ask for written material from the organization before making a contribution.

D. NEVER GIVE OUT YOUR CREDIT CARD NUMBER OVER THE PHONE. Have them send you a bill.

E. NEVER GIVE CASH. Always make your check payable to the charity, not the person collecting the money.

F. WATCH OUT FOR CHARITIES WHOSE NAMES SOUND TOO IMPRESSIVE (the Great American World Charitable Group, for example) or too much like well-known charitable groups (the American Cancer Research Group, the United Way of Giving, etc.).

## REAL SCAM

During the Persian Gulf war, better known as "Desert Storm," telephone scam artists were busy calling people at their homes and asking them to help brave U.S. soldiers in the Gulf pay for telephone calls to their families back home. Targeted homes were asked to pay for the calls with a credit card and were thanked effusively for their patriotism. After all, how could you refuse a request like this—"what are you, a Commie?"

We should never forget the positive side of charitable giving. Most charities are on the level and are genuinely trying to help. The average American household is also trying to help, giving more than $750 to charities each year. Interestingly, lower-income households tend to give a greater percentage of their incomes to charitable causes than their wealthier counterparts. If you aren't already doing so, consider giving something to one or more charities. If you can't spare the cash, give some of your family's used clothing or toys that are still in good shape. You'll get the incredibly good feeling that comes with helping a needy neighbor—and a tax deduction too!

## REAL TIP

Our "friends at the IRS" only allow the deduction of charitable contributions "to the extent allowed by the law." What this means to you is that a $25 contribution to public television, for example, that rewards you with a Bert & Ernie mug worth $10, would allow you to deduct just $15 from your taxable income.

If you're too attached to your stuff, consider joining the 89 million Americans who give some of their time to important causes. You might not get a tax deduction (other than for the miles you actually drive in your car, for example)—but you'll feel "Mahvelous!"

# Keeping Your Job

## "If You're Lucky Enough To Still Have One"

Times are hard. You have no guarantees about job
security—even if you work for a large company that's
shown growth since the turn of the century. I used to
work for Texaco, a company that was proud of its record
of never having laid off an employee. Well, during my ten-
ure with "Big Oil," even Texaco decided that, for the
sake of corporate profitability, some people had to go. It
started with early retirement offerings and then quickly
grew to include actual layoffs. The company's history was
being rewritten right before my eyes.

There are many things you can do to protect your job
and make yourself a more valuable employee. By following these hints you should have more success at work.

## What to Do

### 1. Take Advantage of Training Opportunities

If your company offers any training programs—take
them. If you can find any pertinent outside training

courses, ask your company to pay, or at least contribute
toward, the cost. This may also be an excellent time to
consider getting that MBA, or completing your college
degree. You'll demonstrate to your employer that you're a
team player and, at the same time, make yourself a more
valuable employee. *Note*: Employment experts now agree
that lifetime learning will be the key to job security as we
move into the 1990s and head toward the next millen-
nium.

## 2. Work Harder

This sounds trite, but make sure you get projects done
on time and above your boss's expectations. Always cooperate when the work piles up and be available to help
your boss with any extra work that may have to be done
at night or over the weekend.

## 3. Clip Articles that May Be of Interest to Your Boss and Coworkers

I've been doing this for years and people seem to always
appreciate the thought. Read as many publications and industry journals as you can and look for items that may be
of interest to your boss and coworkers.

## 4. Network Inside Your Company

Stay visible with the people at your own company. It's too
easy to stay in your office and remain focused on your
current assignments day after day. Stay active and maintain positive relationships with all of the people around

you including your bosses and peers. It's much harder for a boss to fire someone who is trying hard every day.

## 5. Don't Be Negative
Bosses hate to see employees speaking badly about the company or—worse—about them. As hard as it can be at times, stay focused, keep your enthusiasm, and try to see the positive side of your company and your coworkers.

---

### REAL SIGNS THAT YOU MAY BE ABOUT TO LOSE YOUR JOB
- You're not invited to meetings.
- You're excluded from memos.
- You're relieved of certain responsibilities.
- Your boss acts differently toward you.
- Your secretary and/or coworkers are acting differently toward you.

### *VERY CLEAR* SIGNS THAT YOUR JOB IS IN DANGER!
- Some of your office furniture is missing!
- Your office lock is changed!
- The nameplate on your door is missing, again!
- Your secretary asks, "What are you doing here?"

---

If you have reason to believe that you're about to lose your job, be sure to follow these important steps:

### 1. SCHEDULE A MEETING WITH YOUR BOSS

Ask for an honest appraisal of your future at the company. If you find that your job is on the line, ask about other opportunities within the company. Under this guilt, your boss may even be willing to help you locate work at another company.

### 2. KEEP YOUR RESUME UP-TO-DATE

Be sure to include your achievements and use language that highlights the contributions you made to your employers.

### 3. MAKE A LIST OF THE PEOPLE WHO MAKE UP YOUR NETWORK

Include friends, coworkers, headhunters, associates at other companies, and anyone else who might be able to help you find work. In the unhappy event that you do get fired, you'll need to call on your network to help you find your next job.

### 4. DON'T TAKE ON ANY NEW DEBT

Wait to buy that new Lexus until your situation gets more secure.

### 5. BUILD UP AN EMERGENCY CASH RESERVE

Put away an amount equal to at least six months of your family's normal expenses. If you find yourself out of work, you can always cut your expenses and make this reserve last even longer.

6. ESTABLISH A HOME EQUITY LINE OF CREDIT
It's easier to do this while you're still working. You may never need it but at least you'll have it available.

7. PREPARE A FAMILY BUDGET
Find any items that could be reduced or even eliminated in the event your paychecks stop coming.

## Dealing With Unemployment

What could be worse than losing your job? Your family gets crazy, your friends act differently around you, neighbors look down when you pass by, and even former work friends ignore you—and talk behind your "fired" back. Even your dog doesn't seem to greet you with the same enthusiasm anymore. You feel like a failure. And you feel like you have nowhere to turn. So what can you do? First of all, relax, and don't get down on yourself. Remember, you're not alone. According to the newsletter *Workplace Trends*, as many as 2,743 Americans lose their jobs each business day. And they're not just talking about assembly line workers and farmhands. The unfortunate group includes marketing executives, sales clerks, and Wall Street commodities traders. At some point during the next twelve months, it is estimated that nearly one in five Americans will find themselves out of work for at least a while.

Long gone are the halcyon days of boundless expansion

and the corporate security blanket. Unlike our fathers, who went off to work each morning to the Very Big Corporation of America, worked hard, earned their vacations, got raises—or maybe even promotions—each year, and looked forward to secure, if somewhat confining, futures, we are operating within a very different reality.

Today, companies rarely think twice before "streamlining" (moving jobs overseas to enjoy the benefits of cheaper nonunion labor), or "downsizing" (firing people to decrease overhead and increase corporate profits) their operations.

To be sure, profits have always been King. But today, a new mind-set seems to have taken hold. Corporate managers, facing the increased pressures of international competition in a new global economy, are unable, or unwilling, to take the feelings and personal circumstances of their employees into account as they plan for the future—a future in which corporate profits must be maximized and their asses saved.

If you find yourself out of work, there are a number of things you'll need to do, and many issues you'll need to consider.

## What to Do

1. MAKE SURE YOU APPLY FOR UNEMPLOYMENT
There's nothing to be ashamed of here. You've paid unemployment taxes for exactly this purpose. Be prepared for

some very long lines, and lengthy processing periods—
at least a few weeks. You'll quickly learn that you aren't
the only one in town who has recently lost his or her
job.

How much you get depends on your past earnings and
the state in which you live. Benefits usually last 26 weeks,
and can reach $400 a week in some states. The bad news:
You'll have to pay taxes on the money you receive.

2. SEE IF YOU CAN STAY ON YOUR COMPANY'S GROUP
HEALTH INSURANCE POLICY UNTIL YOU FIND A NEW JOB
THAT OFFERS INSURANCE

The last thing you want to be doing is worrying about
your family's health insurance as you look for a new job.
If your spouse works, great! You can probably get covered under his or her policy for free, or a small additional
cost. If you were laid off by a company having twenty or
more employees, you're entitled, under the Consolidated
Omnibus Budget Reconciliation Act (COBRA), to stay on
your company's health plan, at your own expense, for up
to eighteen months. They're allowed to charge you a 2%
processing charge, but it's still likely to be a better deal
than you might find elsewhere.

A. HOW DOES IT WORK? Under COBRA, your employer must
notify its insurer within thirty days from the date they
dismiss you. You will then receive a notice from the insurer asking if you want to stay on the company's group
plan. You then have sixty days to respond and accept the
offer. If your company was contributing toward the cost

of your coverage, be ready for higher payments. They're not required to continue paying for any of the costs of your coverage.

B. CAN MY COVERAGE UNDER COBRA BE TERMINATED? Yes. If your old company, in yet another nasty attempt to increase its profitability, stops providing health insurance for its remaining employees, you'll lose your coverage too. You'll also lose your right to coverage if you obtain insurance under another policy or become eligible for Medicare. *Note:* COBRA is a good law. My wife and I were able to continue with our group coverage after I "parted ways" with a former employer. Some states have instituted modifications to COBRA, so be sure to check with your company's benefits coordinator.

3. SEE IF YOUR COMPANY PROVIDES
OUT-PLACEMENT COUNSELING
Many companies, usually acting out of guilt, not philanthropy, offer laid-off employees the services of a staff counselor, or pay for all or part of the expense of private placement counseling. Ask what services you're entitled to.

4. ESTABLISH A ROUTINE
It's important to have a reason to get up every morning. Some who have been laid off start an exercise regimen or schedule regular early meetings. The key here is to avoid any self-pity, or suffer any loss of momentum.

### 5. USE YOUR TIME CONSTRUCTIVELY

Research other companies in your field and related business areas. Who knows, you may end up finding a better job or switching to a career that's better suited to your skills and interests. Wouldn't it be great to actually thank your old boss for letting you go!

### 6. CONSIDER PART-TIME OR TEMPORARY WORK

Many companies, in yet another attempt to save money, are turning to outside consultants (cynically, of course, since they don't have to provide consultants with benefits). Your old company is a good place to start. Also check with your company's suppliers and clients. Part-time or temporary work can easily become full-time when the economy improves, the company's fortunes grow, or you prove yourself to be invaluable.

### 7. NETWORK

Alert all of your business contacts that you are looking for a position. Schedule as many informational interviews as you can. Even if there is "no job at the present time," a person who actually sees you face to face is much more likely to remember you when something does become available. Ask for names of other people in their company, or at other companies, who would be willing to speak with you.

### 8. FOLLOW UP ON YOUR MEETINGS

Always send a note thanking your contact for his or her time. Promise to check in by phone every two to three

weeks to keep that person up-to-date on your progress.
This makes members of your network allies in your
search for a new job. If you succeed, they too will feel
like they've succeeded.

---

### TAX TIP

Remember to keep all your receipts and records of job-
hunting and training expenses—they're tax-deductible.

---

### 9. CONTACT PLACEMENT FIRMS
### ("HEADHUNTERS") IN YOUR FIELD

Headhunters tend to focus on specific career paths and
levels of positions so be sure to approach them with a
very clear idea of the kind of position you're seeking.

### 10. CONTACT YOUR HIGH SCHOOL, UNIVERSITY,
### OR GRADUATE SCHOOL FOR ASSISTANCE

Many schools have full-time career counselors who will
help you in your search for employment. On more than
one occasion, I've used my graduate school's placement
office to secure consulting work. You can also check with
your state or county human resources offices to see what
services they offer.

### 11. JOIN A PROFESSIONAL ASSOCIATION

Meetings are an excellent place to meet your peers and
find out about new job openings. Some associations even

have placement committees that help unemployed members.

## 12. JOIN OR START A SUPPORT GROUP

It can be very helpful and informative to meet with peers in similar situations. Check your local newspaper for meetings, or call your local library, continuing education provider, or YMCA.

## 13. AVOID FEE-FOR-SERVICE JOB PLACEMENT SERVICES

Most legitimate placement companies are paid by the hiring company, although a few may ask that you pay at least part of the fee, but only after they've placed you in a job. Temporary agencies are also normally paid a prearranged amount by the hiring company. You receive your paychecks from the agency, not the company where you are actually doing the work.

---

### REAL WARNING

Watch out for any placement companies that ask for money up front or require a fee before actually placing you in a job. Also avoid any "900" numbers that promise "high-paying jobs in your field," or offer the "ten secrets to career success." You'll most likely get less than you paid for.

---

If you have any doubts about an employment agency or career counseling service, contact your local department of consumer affairs, your state attorney general's office or your local Better Business Bureau before you get involved.

14. DON'T BE A VICTIM OF WORK-AT-HOME SCAMS—
EVEN IF YOU CAN "MAKE $3,000 EACH WEEK IN
YOUR SPARE TIME."

As your mother always warned you—or should have if she didn't—"If it sounds too good to be true, it probably is." So what's the catch? Well, for one you'll probably have to pay this too-good-to-be-true employer something in advance, maybe to pay for your equipment or supplies, before you can start making the "big money." You may never recoup this "investment," let alone make thousands of dollars in your spare time.

15. STAY IN TOUCH WITH YOUR NETWORK

Even—especially!—after you've found a new job. You never know when you'll need to contact these people again. You may even hear from one of them in the future regarding other opportunities. Networking should begin while you're looking for your first job and never end.

## Money Trouble

If things get rough, and you're actually in danger of running out of money, you may have to resort to one or more of the following options:

## 1. BORROW AGAINST YOUR HOME

If you have any equity in your home, you may be able to borrow against it. Best strategy: In the expectation of a possible layoff (you usually have some warning), establish a home equity line of credit. It's much easier to qualify for a loan while you're still working.

## 2. BORROW AGAINST YOUR CASH VALUE LIFE INSURANCE

While experts generally advise against this type of insurance, you may own a policy that you bought BEFORE you started reading this book. If so, remember that you can borrow against the equity you've accumulated in your policy.

## 3. TAP INTO YOUR RETIREMENT ACCOUNT(S)

You'll pay taxes on the money, and a 10% penalty, but it may be your only option. *Warning*: Some retirement accounts restrict borrowing.

## 4. BORROW MONEY FROM RELATIVES
## (WHO WON'T NEED THE MONEY BACK SOON)

Establish a payment plan that keeps you in the pattern of paying "something" back each month, even if you have to borrow more later. *Note*: Make sure your relationship can handle this strain. Many families can get real strange about money. If this is true of your family, move on to . . .

## 5. STOP PAYING THE FULL AMOUNT ON YOUR BILLS

Notify your creditors of your predicament and offer to pay some small amount each month. Always pay something, and work to make your creditors allies in your fight to get back on track. It may actually work, at least for a while.

---

## REAL ADVICE

You should make every attempt to stay current with your insurance bills. Health insurance may be expensive, but without it you're vulnerable to a health, and financial, catastrophe. Life insurance policies can be hard to reinstate if you let them lapse.

---

### 6. MOVE TO LESS EXPENSIVE HOUSING
### OR A LESS EXPENSIVE REGION

In my opinion, this should definitely be an option of last resort. Moving is likely to upset and disrupt your family more than any other single action you can take. If you are forced to take this step, consider renting your home and moving in with relatives until you get back on your feet. It's not quite as permanent as a move and you'll be able to return to your own home when you're able.

# CREDIT:
## Staying Out of Trouble

---

## Credit Cards

---

How many TV sit-coms can you remember where the sit-com wife is yelled at once again by her sit-com husband for spending too much with her credit card? And whether you remember it being Lucy and Ricky, Alice and Ralph, or even Wilma and Fred, the point is: Life imitates art (or is it art imitates life?). And while America's gender prejudices may have tempered somewhat over the years, our love of spending—and credit spending in particular—has grown like the hole in the ozone layer.

To be sure, there are some good reasons to have credit cards:

- They can help you establish a credit record— assuming you make your payments on time.
- They can be good in emergencies when you may not have ready access to cash.
- They're convenient.
- They make it much easier to rent a car.
- They allow you to purchase concert tickets or other merchandise over the phone.

- They're safer than cash.
- They allow for extended payments.
- They provide a record of purchases.
- They can provide extra protection (warranties on purchases, travel insurance, etc.).

On the other hand, credit cards allow material-hungry Americans to enjoy instant gratification, even when they might not be able to afford it. The result is a record $231 billion in outstanding credit charges and a record low 28% of cardholders who pay their credit card accounts in full each month.

Credit card issuers make more than 80% of their money from your interest payments. Credit cards may not be the pariah that many consumer groups make them out to be, but they do need to be handled with extreme care.

## 1. Shopping For a Credit Card

Credit cards come in many flavors and styles. In order to obtain the card that's right for you, you'll need to assess your own situation and consider the following options:

### A. REVOLVING-CREDIT CARDS

Also known as bank cards, RCs account for the largest share of credit card spending today. They're also the most dangerous.

*Beware:* Revolving-credit cards can be as dangerous as a plastic explosive. These cards, sponsored by banks and other financial organizations, and managed by clearinghouses like Visa and MasterCard, allow you to carry an outstanding balance indefinitely, so long as you make a small minimum payment each month. For their trouble, the companies usually charge you an annual fee and interest on your outstanding balance—anywhere from 10.5% to 24%, but averaging almost 19%.

## B. TRAVEL AND ENTERTAINMENT CARDS
The best-known T&E cards available today are offered by American Express, Diners Club, and Carte Blanche.

*Disadvantage:* These cards require payment in full each month. *Advantage:* These cards require you to pay your balance in full each month—you won't fall behind on your payments and become one more victim of excessive interest charges. T&E cards are best for frequent travelers and business people who need a large credit line to pay for airline tickets, hotels, and other large expenses. The main drawback to these cards is their relatively high annual fees, which can be as much as several hundred dollars.

## C. DEPARTMENT STORE CARDS
Similar in structure to RCs, department store cards are issued, as common sense would dictate, by department stores.

*Warning:* While department store cards are easier to obtain, and may waive any annual fee, they usually charge higher interest rates. They might also work psychologically—that's what they count on—to encourage cardholders to shop at that particular store. Avoid these if you can. You can always use your revolving-credit card to shop at your favorite department store.

### D. GASOLINE/OIL COMPANY CARDS

Really just another type of T&E card, gas and oil company cards allow you to purchase gas, oil, repairs, and other goods and services from their outlets, provided you pay your balance in full each month. Some companies do offer a revolving-credit option and some even offer special services like travel insurance, check cashing, and emergency cash. In general, these cards offer lower rates than bank cards, but be sure to compare their rates, fees, and services before signing on.

### E. SECURED CARDS

Secured credit cards are geared toward individuals with credit problems or no borrowing history. They are available from many of the same institutions that offer ordinary RCs. Cardholders put up a deposit and can then charge goods and services up to approximately that amount. After a period of time, during which you regularly pay your bills and stay out of any other credit trouble, you can generate a favorable credit record and then apply for an unsecured card.

If you go for a secured card, you should receive interest on your deposit, so be sure to ask for the issuer's rate. Also ask about minimum deposits, finance charges, annual fees, any special application or processing fees, and the time required before you can convert to an unsecured card.

## F. AFFINITY CARDS

A growing player in the credit card arena, affinity cards are little more than a clever marketing gimmick. These revolving-credit cards contribute a small percentage of your charges, usually .25% to .50% to certain charitable organizations. In some cases, they also donate a portion of your annual fee or a percentage of the interest you pay on any outstanding balances. Some affinity cards even offer cardholders frequent flier miles or discounts on baseball tickets.

*Personal Note:* I just received a credit card offer in the mail today from my alma mater: No annual fee, a *"low* 17.9%" annual percentage rate, and the choice of a Visa Classic or Visa Gold card. What's more, I get to help fund programs at the school and display with pride the logo of my undergraduate university during every purchase. However, they didn't make mention of the exact amount to be given to the school, and their 2% charge for any cash advances is only mentioned in very small print on the back of the application form.

Whatever the enticements, you have to compare affinity cards on the basis of their fees, rates, contributions, and other services. With today's average cardholder charging about $2,000 each year, the average affinity card would provide just about $10 per cardholder to charitable groups.

## REAL RIP-OFF

While it might make you feel good to know that your credit card is generating contributions to certain charitable causes that you believe in—the Elvis Presley Memorial Foundation in the case of the Elvis MasterCard, for example—remember that you may not deduct any portion of this contribution from YOUR taxes. Only the credit card company benefits from the tax deduction. *Better Stragegy*: Shop for the best card available and then make any charitable contributions on your own.

G. PREMIUM CARDS

Silver cards, gold cards, even platinum cards. What's next? Caviar cards? Diamond cards? BEWARE: These cards are one part substance and one part image. Make certain that their "enhancements" are worth the extra cost, as much as $100 in some cases. While a platinum card may make you feel more powerful than your child's favorite superhero, research shows that fewer than 10% of cardholders actually make significant use of these extra benefits. Some of the extra services these cards may offer include:

- Higher credit limits (often available with any card).
- Roadside assistance (usually just locates a towing company and bills you for the garage's bill).
- Purchase protection on new merchandise (available on many regular cards).
- Extended warranties (available on some basic cards).

- Emergency access to cash (most do this if you apply through a bank).
- Travel insurance (many regular cards offer this if you charge the trip with their card but premium cards often offer higher levels of coverage).
- Rental car insurance (included with many basic cards and often unnecessary depending on your personal auto policy).

## 2. Comparison-Shopping

With each type of credit card, there are many important differences to consider. You'll need to pay close attention as you shop around. Organizations like the Bankcard Holders of America (560 Herndon Parkway, Suite 120, Herndon, VA 22070, 703-481-1110) can help in your search. Also check *Money* magazine and *Kiplinger's Personal Finance* for listings of current bargains. When shopping for a card, remember to consider the following points:

### A. HOW MUCH IS THE *ANNUAL FEE*?

Many cards now waive their annual fee during some initial period, usually six months or a year. Find out how much the fee will be *after* this promotional period has ended. If you're one of those people who are smart enough to pay off your outstanding balance each month, a no-fee card is probably your best bet (the interest rate won't matter).

### B. WHAT IS THE *INTEREST RATE*?

Most revolving-credit cards charge a fixed rate of interest. Find out what this rate is and watch out for any hid-

den introductory rates or variable rates that could shoot
up after an initial "teaser period." If you're one of the
growing number of people who carry an outstanding
balance on your card, shop for the lowest possible rate.

Also, ask how the interest is calculated. Companies
can calculate interest based on your balance at the beginning of each period, the end of each period, or on
your monthly average balance. This may make a significant difference in your payments. *Note:* Credit card interest payments are NO LONGER TAX-DEDUCT-
IBLE.

*Worth trying:* If you've been a good boy or girl—paid your
bills on time—you can try to get your credit card company to reduce your interest rate or even waive the annual fee. More companies are saying yes to these
requests out of fear of losing good customers. It never
hurts to ask. If they don't play ball, shop around for another card.

C. WHAT IS THE *GRACE PERIOD*?
This is the period of time from the date your bill is sent
out to the time they start charging you interest. In general, grace periods range anywhere from 21 to 30 days.
Look for a grace period of at least 25 days.

D. IS THERE A CHARGE FOR *CASH ADVANCES*?
Some companies gouge you for as much as a 2% fee on
any cash advances. Try to find a card that doesn't charge
extra for this service.

E. DOES THE CARD PROVIDE ANY *SPECIAL SERVICES*?

Things like warranty protection, travel insurance, or annual transaction summaries may be important to you. In general, however, these services will only be available on cards with higher annual fees.

---

**REAL TIP**

If you belong to a credit union, check to see if they offer a credit card. Credit unions often offer better rates and fees than banks. To find out if you're eligible to join a credit union, call the Credit Union National Association at 608-231-4044.

---

IMPORTANT CAUTIONS:

1. Beware of preapproved credit cards that arrive in the mail. Many of these offers have hidden fees or try to charge you interest on your preapproved credit line. Also, don't just throw these cards in the garbage. Cut them in half and return the remains to the issuing company. Otherwise, your credit report may show an open line of credit, making it harder for you to get credit when you need it.

2. Never pay to apply for a credit card. No matter how bad your credit problems may be, NEVER call one of those 900-FOR-CREDIT services advertised on late-night television. Not only will you pay handsomely for the 900 number call, but you'll pay an up-front fee for their service—if they ever follow through on your application.

## 3. Resolving Problems

### A. BILLING ERRORS

With any luck, you'll never have to deal with a billing error on your credit card. If you do, however, be certain to follow these steps:

1. ACT WITHIN SIXTY DAYS. The federal Fair Credit Billing Act (FCBA) requires that complaints be made in writing within sixty days of the mailing date of your statement.

---

### REAL MISTAKE

Just calling your card's customer service department. Even though someone may promise with all his or her heart to resolve the problem and get back to you, you can lose critical time while this person does or does not act on your call. You'll also have no record of your complaint and nothing in writing to show for your trouble.

---

2. PUT YOUR COMPLAINT IN WRITING. Include detailed information and keep a copy of the letter. Send your letter to the issuer by registered or certified mail with a return receipt requested.

3. FOLLOW UP ON YOUR COMPLAINT. The credit card issuer is required to resolve your problem within ninety days, either with a correction or a detailed explanation of why they feel no billing error has occured.

If they say you're wrong and no billing error has occured, you can either:

- Pay the bill.
- Contact your state attorney general's office and ask
  for assistance.
- Withhold payment, and risk being sued by the credit
  card company and having your credit record tar-
  nished.
- As a last resort, you can contact the company's com-
  pliance officer and threaten to sue.

*To find out more* about your rights under the Fair Credit
Billing Act, contact the Federal Trade Commission (offices in Washington, D.C., and many larger cities) or call
the Bankcard Holders of America at 703-481-1110.

### B. STOLEN CARDS

If you happen to believe what Karl Malden says in his
commercials, the chance of having your wallet or purse
stolen the next time you leave home is about 99.9%. If you
simply choose to believe current police statistics instead,
the chances of this happening to you at any point in your
lifetime may be pretty good. *WHAT TO DO?* Don't worry
and don't panic. Just call your issuer's 800 number and
report your card as stolen.

### C. DEBT TROUBLE

It's not hard to get into trouble with credit cards—anyone
can do it. Who can resist the temptation to buy whatever
they want without paying for it until, well, whenever. In

general, your monthly installment debt (credit cards, car loans, etc.), not including housing, should be less than 20% of your take-home pay.

If you do get into trouble, and you can't seem to catch up with your credit card bills, DO NOT:

- Leave the country.
- Use yet another card to pay off the others, unless it has a substantially lower interest rate and doesn't charge a fee for cash advances.
- Pay money to a lawyer or a private credit repair organization.
- Consider bankruptcy, at least until all other measures have failed.

BETTER IDEAS:

1. Write a letter to your issuer(s) stating your problem. They'll probably meet with you to discuss the situation and set up a payment plan that you can handle. Remember, they'd rather have you paying something than be closed out if you declare bankruptcy.

2. Contact a not-for-profit credit counseling service in your community. They often can help and they won't ask for any payment up front. These agencies are more likely to have success in their attempts to negotiate with your creditors. One source of help is the National Foundation for Consumer Credit (301) 589-5600. Another is the Consumer Credit Counseling National Referral Line (1-800-388-2227). They can direct you to a nearby counseling service.

## REAL WISDOM

A wise man, or maybe it was just my eighth grade English teacher, once said to me, and I will never forget this, "Heymann; when in doubt, leave it out." He was talking about commas, of course, but this same wisdom can easily be applied to credit cards: If you don't really need to use them, don't. Like commas, and fast cars and fast friends, credit cards can be much more trouble than they're worth.

# Debit Cards

As we approach our destiny as a cashless society, debit cards are playing an ever-expanding role. Debit cards, like credit cards, can be used in place of cash to buy goods and services. Unlike credit cards, however, debit card purchases draw cash instantly from your bank account or, in the case of Visa's or MasterCard's debit cards, within a few days. You do not have a revolving-credit option.

ADVANTAGES:
- You don't have to carry large amounts of cash.
- You don't have to hassle with writing checks.
- You can stay on a budget more easily since you can't charge more than you have in the bank.

DISADVANTAGES:
- You must have the funds available at the time of the purchase.

- You lose the free grace period that comes with a credit card.
- You can be charged a per-transaction fee. Ask your bank.

## Credit Reports

A great deal of fuss has been made recently over credit reports and the bureaus that compile and distribute them for a fee. While businesses depend on these bureaus and their reports to size up potential customers, a great number of consumers have been their unwitting victims. According to the advocacy group Consumer's Union, nearly 50% of credit reports contain some inaccurate information, and nearly 20% have at least one major inaccuracy.

### 1. WHAT THIS MEANS TO YOU

If you're seeking credit for the purchase of a car, a mortgage on a home, or just applying for a credit card, you could be refused credit and lose your chance to make a deal with that lender; all because of something that may not be your fault.

### 2. WHAT YOU CAN DO

The Fair Credit Reporting Act (FCRA) requires credit bureaus to provide easy access to credit files. Check your credit file on a regular basis, at least every year and more often if you are anticipating a major purchase. Fees range from $3 to $20 depending on the reporting company and the state in which you live. If you're applying for joint credit with your spouse, you'll have to check both of your individual credit files. Your spouse may have failed to pay off a student loan or may have some other black mark related to his or her sordid past.

If you're denied credit, insurance, or even employment because of a negative credit report, you're entitled to receive a free copy of your file from that reporting company, provided that you apply within thirty days. Acting in anticipation of legislation that will provide interested consumers with free reports on an annual basis, at least one major company, TRW, now provides one free report to consumers each year. Take advantage of this offer.

If you're anticipating a major purchase, or planning to apply for credit for any reason, check your credit file before you apply. If there's a black mark on your record, you'll have the opportunity to correct it before you lose your dreamhouse or suffer the embarrassment of a rejection on a new car loan.

Close any existing credit lines that are not being used. Even though you may have a zero balance on your fifteenth low-rate credit card, a lender will count that credit line against you as if it were fully extended. Why? You could take on that much additional credit if you wanted.

3. WHO ARE THESE PEOPLE?

There are three major credit bureaus operating in the United States today: TRW, Equifax, and Trans Union. Together, these bureaus, along with 800 or 900 smaller players, maintain nearly 400 million individual credit files. It's probably a good idea to request your file from all three major companies since businesses may receive reports on your history from any one of them.

4. WHAT KIND OF INFORMATION DO THEY HAVE?
It's not quite *1984* time, but some good clean paranoia may be warranted. These companies know a lot about you and your spending habits. Some of the things "Big Brother" knows about YOU include:
- Your current and past residences.
- Your Social Security number.
- Your employment history.
- Personal information regarding your marriages, divorces, judgments, arrests, convictions, and other matters of public record.
- Your credit lines and maximum balances on those accounts.
- Your payment history (including any late payments).
- Your current balances.
- Any accounts that were referred to collection agencies.
- Any repossessions, tax liens, or bankruptcies.

*Note:* Information regarding your reputation or chosen lifestyle are not supposed to appear on a standard credit report.

5. ACCESS TO YOUR CREDIT FILE
Supposedly, only businesses with a "permissible purpose" are allowed to see your credit file. Defining what is

"permissible" has not yet been attempted, so assume that pretty much anyone with your address and Social Security number can gain access to your credit history. Your credit file will show if and when any inquiries were made about your credit history, and who made the requests. Inquiries must be kept on file for at least six months if they concern a credit application and two years in the case of an employment application.

---

REAL ABUSE: Many credit reporting agencies rent names from their computer files to credit card companies and other direct marketers.

REAL SOLUTION: Write to the three major credit bureaus and ask to be removed from their rental lists:
- TRW National Consumer Assistance Center
  12606 Greenville Avenue. P.O. Box 749029
  Dallas, TX 75374-9029
  714-385-7000
- Equifax Credit Information Services
  P.O. Box 9095
  Farmingdale, NY 11735
  404-885-8000
- Trans Union
  1211 Chestnut Street
  Philadelphia, PA 19107
  312-431-5100

---

6. CREDIT FILE ERRORS

You're going to have to "get busy" on this one. The "average consumer" spends twenty-three weeks trying to

correct a credit file inaccuracy BEFORE finally going to
the Federal Trade Commission.

Some common mistakes made on credit files include:
* Being confused with another person with the same
  last name.
* Being confused with another person who previously
  lived at the same address.
* Having incorrect data placed into your record.

The list goes on and on. In one notable case, an entire
town was placed in credit purgatory when a credit bureau
incorrectly recorded all of their accounts as having tax
liens. You have to monitor these guys very carefully.
*Good News*: A great deal of legislation is pending that will
force credit bureaus to clean up their act.

7. IF YOU FIND AN ERROR ON YOUR CREDIT FILE:
You should first write to the credit bureau and explain
why your record is inaccurate. Send your letter by registered or certified mail (return receipt requested) and
keep a copy. Include any information that supports your
case. They're required to get back to you within thirty
days with the results of their investigation.

IF THEY DECIDE THAT YOU'RE CORRECT: The bureau must remove the incorrect information from your file. Make certain that they do this. Also, check to make sure that the
information is cleared from the files of other credit bureaus. If you request it, the credit bureau must notify all

parties who have seen the inaccurate information within the past six months of the correction.

IF THEY DECIDE THAT YOU'RE WRONG: You have the right to add your side of the story to the record. As a result, your version of the story will also be presented when your credit history is requested. Even with negative information on your record, a statement from you is allowable and may help with potential lenders or employers.

## Establishing Credit

First of all, if you don't already have one, open a checking or savings account with a bank, preferably one that has a Visa or MasterCard program. These accounts may not show up on your credit file but they can be used to show that you have some money in the bank and your cancelled checks will prove that you pay your bills on a regular basis. If you're a good boy or girl, i.e., don't write any rubber checks, you may be able to get a credit card directly from that bank in a relatively short period of time.

Second, apply for a gasoline or department store credit card. These are the easiest to qualify for. Make sure that the companies you apply to report their accounts to credit reporting agencies on a regular basis. Remember: You're trying to establish a positive credit history. Paying your bills on time to a firm that doesn't report your stellar behavior to the major credit reporting agencies won't help much. Do you remember this philosophical question?: If a tree falls in the forest and nobody hears it, does it really make a sound?

If you're accepted for one of these cards, go out and buy some merchandise—*weeeee!*—but be sure to pay your bills on time—*whhhhhhhhooooooooo!*

If these tactics don't work, apply for a *secured credit card.*

As a last resort, ask someone to cosign your credit card application. Then make charges and pay your bills on time. After a period of a few months, or in some cases as much as a year, you can apply for an individual unsecured credit card.

## REAL TIP

While you're trying to establish a credit history, DO NOT apply for credit from as many different sources as you can in order to "improve your chances." Every time a potential lender checks your credit history, that inquiry goes into your credit file. If you have tons of inquiries, a potential lender may get scared off.

## Credit Problems

A bad credit record can limit your access to housing, credit, insurance, and even employment. Unfortunately, whether as the result of errors or actual payment problems, more Americans are finding themselves in this impaired position.

*What to do?:* First of all, work hard to repair your credit and reestablish your credit-worthiness. A basic Q&A:

*Question:* How long do you have to live with black marks on your credit file?

*Answer:* Negative entries can remain in your file for as long as seven years, bankruptcies for ten. Some businesses that request your file may scan only the past few years—but you shouldn't assume that this will be the case.

## 1. Watch Out For Credit Repair Companies

Credit repair firms claim they can clear your credit record of any black marks and give you back your good name. Sounds attractive! You may even think to yourself, "Maybe I will call that 900 number I just saw advertised during "Leave it to Beaver." DON'T DO IT! The only thing you're likely to gain by calling 900-EZ-CREDIT is an oversized charge on your next phone bill.

*Warning:* Many of these companies are not on the level.

No one can clear your credit record of legitimate black marks, legally that is. As far as errors on your record are concerned, you can fight for your rights just as well as these companies. Also **DO NOT**:

A. USE A FINANCE COMPANY TO CONSOLIDATE YOUR DEBTS
Even if they do call themselves "The E-Z Money Store,"
you'll pay heavily in the end for the privilege of borrowing some of their "merchandise."

B. USE A BILL-PAYING SERVICE TO MAKE
YOUR MONTHLY PAYMENTS
If you had the money, you could pay your bills yourself.
These firms charge you a fee, often as high as 10% of
your monthly payments, to pay your bills for you—with
your money. It's simply a pricy check-writing service.

C. APPLY FOR AS MUCH CREDIT AS YOU CAN
"IN CASE THE DOORS ARE CLOSED ON YOU LATER"
Credit can be revoked. And ask yourself, "Isn't this what
got me into trouble in the first place?"

D. MOVE DURING THE NIGHT AND
CHANGE YOUR FACIAL IDENTITY
Your credit history follows you everywhere.

## 2. What You *Can* Do

You CAN repair your credit. Depending on your situation,
it may take some time. But be patient, persevere, and follow these steps:

A. GET A COPY OF YOUR CREDIT REPORT
See what the problems actually are. You may find that
some of your mistakes, "childhood indiscretions" if you
will, may have never been reported—the perfect crime.

B. TAKE STEPS TO REMOVE ANY INACCURATE INFORMATION

C. ADD A STATEMENT TO YOUR FILE
Do this while you're contesting any errors or if you have a legitimate explanation for previous credit problems. You're entitled to add up to hundred words.

D. PAY OFF ANY OUTSTANDING COLLECTIONS, ACCOUNTS, LIENS, OR JUDGMENTS.
If you're in a dispute with a business, make every attempt to resolve it. Work with a not-for-profit credit counseling agency to help you get back on track. Call the National Foundation for Consumer Credit, Inc. at 301-589-5600 for an office near you.

E. GET RID OF ANY EXCESS CREDIT
Keep only the cards or credit lines in which you have balances, or may need for an emergency. *Note*: A possible late-breaking sale at Macy's does not qualify as an emergency.

# Bankruptcy

We've all done it—maybe only while playing Monopoly—but how bad can it be to declare bankruptcy in REAL life? As the experts will tell you, and as the nearly one million Americans who do it each year should know, bankruptcy should absolutely be your last resort. As you will see in this section, bankruptcy can stay with you like a bad meal, a ten-year bad meal.

Nonetheless, bankruptcy may be your best, and probably your only option, if and when all efforts to reach some agreement with your creditors have failed.

Before you take this drastic step, however, contact your creditors and ask for mercy. They may be willing to consider a reasonable monthly payment plan. Use a not-for-profit credit counseling service, and not a private percentage-based service, in your locality. If you don't know of one, contact the National Foundation for Consumer Credit at 301-589-5600. They will put you in touch with a consumer credit counseling service (CCCS) in your area. A credit counseling service will probably fare better than you with your lenders. Avoid any for-profit credit counseling companies. They'll charge you a hefty fee—in advance.

*Beware:* Many lenders will be tough. They may agree to reduce your monthly payments, but at a higher interest rate and over a greater period of time. You may be selling your soul to the devil just to gain a little more time. But if your debts are just too big to handle—and you can't get a Trump-sized loan from a benevolent relative— you may just have to concede and consider the *"B"* word.

# Pick Your Poison: Forms of Bankruptcy

CHAPTER 13

The preferred form of personal bankruptcy (that's like talking about the preferred method of root canal), chapter 13 of the bankruptcy code allows you to keep your property while you agree to a court-approved plan to repay at least some of your debts. This option is usually reserved for individuals with relatively small amounts of debt and some chance of repaying.

CHAPTER 7

Less lenient than 13, but more commonly practiced, chapter 7 of the bankruptcy code may cancel at least some of your debts, including certain credit card charges. *Problem*: You'll probably have to give up title to at least some of your beloved property although in most states homes and cars are generally excluded from seizure. Chapter 7 is typically used by debtors with the least assets and the slimmest chance of repayment.

CHAPTER 11

No it's "not just for businesses anymore." Individuals are now allowed to enjoy the glory of filing for chapter 11 protection from their creditors. This form of bankruptcy usually makes sense only if you have large assets at stake. Since your creditors must approve your repayment plan, this approach can be time-consuming and expensive.

CHAPTER 20

A hybrid of chapters 13 and 7 of the bankruptcy code, chapter 20 bankruptcy ("13" plus "7" equals 20) allows you to eliminate certain debts under the chapter 7 provisions and then set up a repayment plan under chapter 13. While this may sound attractive, you're actually filing for bankruptcy twice so you'll have to pay two filing fees and incur additional lawyers' fees. Also, this structure is not permissable in every state.

Remember, bankruptcy can stay on your credit record for up to ten years, and you may be asked about it beyond that. You'll almost certainly face a great deal of trouble when you try to get credit again. A majority of bankruptcy filers have to wait more than five years to secure any new credit, and mortgages are generally out of the question.

You'll need to contact a lawyer before filing for any form of bankruptcy. Don't worry about the welfare of your mouthpiece. He or she will charge you anywhere from $400 to $1,500, payable in advance if they can get it. At worst, they'll move to the front of your creditor line if and when anyone gets paid. You'll also have to pay a filing fee, usually just over $100. All in all it's a pretty expensive process for someone who's supposed to be broke.

# INDEX

Accelerated death benefits, 89, 148–149

Accessory apartments, 136, 161–162

Adjustable-rate mortgages, 56, 65, 67–69, 80

Adult care facilities, 166–167

Adult day care, 163

Adult homes, 166–167

Affinity credit cards, 267–268

Airbags, 11, 115

Alzheimer's disease, 152, 153

A.M. Best, 94, 123

American Association of Homes for the Aging (AAHA), 138, 165–166

American Association of Retired Persons (AARP), 138, 147, 159, 162

American Council of Life Insurance, 91

American Express, 221, 265

American Institute of Real Estate Appraisers, The, 37

American Medical Association (AMA), 43

American Society of Home Inspectors (ASHI), 40

Annual Percentage Rate (APR), 65, 74, 180, 181

Annual Renewable Term life insurance, 85, 89–93

Antilock brakes, 11, 115

Antitheft devices, 115, 117

Apartments for independent living, 166–167

Application fee (mortgage), 76

Appraisals, 37–38, 76, 105, 106

Area Agencies on Aging (AAA), 137–138

Asbestos, 43–44

Asset allocation, 190–191, 193

Assisted living facilities,
169
Auctions, 49
Auto insurance, 11–12, 20,
22, 100, 110–117
Automatic seat belts, 115

Baccalaureate bonds, 207
Bait-and-Switch scam,
231
Bankcard Holders of America,
269, 273
Bank credit cards, 264–265,
281
Bank money market funds,
183
Bankruptcy, 274, 285–288
Banks, 184
Better Business Bureau, 4, 21,
23, 42, 56, 226, 233, 235,
243, 246, 260
Bill-paying services, 284
Bi-weekly mortgages, 70
Blue Cross/Blue Shield, 124,
147
Board and care homes,
167–169
Boarders, 161
Bonds, 187–191, 196
Brokers, mortgage, 61–62
Burglar alarms, 110
Burial, 129

Buyer protection programs,
41
Buying a car (*see* Car buying)
Buying a home (*see* Home
buying)

*Car Book, The* (Gillis), 4
Car buying, 3–24
  dealerships, 4
  deposits, 14
  financing, 12, 15–17, 73,
  223–224
  leasing, 17–19
  maintenance, 4, 12, 16–17,
  23
  model shuffle, 9–10
  negotiations, 12–14
  options, 11–12, 14
  price information, 4, 7, 9–11
  price quotes, 13
  salespeople, 5–8
  showrooms, 6–7
  sticker prices, 10–11
  test drives, 5, 23
  trade-ins, 12, 13, 15, 17
  used cars, 21–24
  warranties, 12, 19–20, 24
Career counseling services,
258, 259
Care managers, 157
Car insurance (*see* Auto
insurance)

Carte Blanche, 265
Car thefts, 111, 115
Cash, 215–216, 223
Cash advances, 270
Cash value life insurance,
    87–88, 90, 261
CDs (certificates of deposit),
    185–186, 191, 196, 207
Charities, 244–248
Charles Schwab, 196
Chartered Financial
    Consultants, 194
Chartered Life Insurance
    Underwriters (CLUs),
    93
Checks, 216–219
Children of Aging Parents
    (CAPS), 138, 160
Civil service disability
    benefits, 100
Classic Residences, 169
Closing costs, 28, 29, 59, 65,
    72, 74–80, 179
Coinsurance, 122
Collectibles, 188
College Board, 206
College tuition, 176–177,
    203–208
Collision damage, 111, 114
Collision damage waiver
    (CDW), 112
Commodity futures, 188

Community resources for
    elderly, 162–165
Companions, 161
Comparison shopping, 13,
    110, 123–124, 180,
    269–271
*Complete Guide to Used Cars*
    (Consumer Guide), 23
Comprehensive car damage,
    111, 114
Condominiums, 46–47,
    104
Congregate housing, 167
Consolidated Omnibus
    Budget Reconciliation
    Act (COBRA), 121, 123,
    255, 256
Consumer Credit Counseling
    National Referral Line,
    274
Consumer Guide, 23
Consumer Reports, 4, 10, 15,
    23, 91
Consumer's Union, 276
Continuing care retirement
    communities (CCRCs),
    141, 169–172
Conventional mortgages,
    58
Cooling off regulations, 217
Co-ops, 47
Corporate bonds, 187

Cost-of-living adjustments
(COLAs), 95, 151, 210,
211
Coupons, 231
Credit, establishing,
281–282
Credit cards, 178, 180–181,
219–221, 243, 247,
263–275
affinity, 267–268
comparison shopping,
269–271
department store, 265–266,
281
gasoline/oil company, 266,
281
premium, 268–269
resolving problems,
272–274
revolving, 264–265, 281
secured, 266–267, 282
travel and entertainment,
265
Credit counseling services,
274, 286
Credit problems, 61, 282–285
Credit reports, 61, 77,
276–281, 284–285
Credit Union National
Association, 271
Credit unions, 62, 184, 271

Custodial care, 144, 147–153,
172

Dealerships, 4
Debit cards, 222, 275–276
Debt trouble, 61, 273–274,
282–285
Deductibles, 121, 122, 124,
143
Deed of assets, 141
Deferred contingent sales
charge, 200
Dental care, 144
Department store credit
cards, 265–266, 281
Dependent care credit,
161
Deposits, 14
Diners Club, 265
Direct Marketing Association,
233, 234, 238, 239, 241
Disability insurance, 97–102,
119
Discounts, 16
*DoAble Renewable Home, The*
(American Association of
Retired Persons), 159
Doctor visits, 118, 143
Dollar cost averaging,
191–192
Double indemnity clause, 95

Downpayments, 58, 79
Downsizing, 254
Dread disease policies, 119
Durable powers of attorney, 141
Dying intestate, 131

Earnings, verification of, 61
Earthquake insurance, 104
ECHO (Elder Cottage Housing Opportunity) housing, 136, 162
*Edmund's Used Car Prices*, 15, 23
Effective annual yield, 183
Elder Law Attorney, 142
Elderly relatives, 135–175
  assistance groups, 137–139
  community resources, 162–165
  financial arrangements, 139–142
  health care, 135–136, 142–147
  home care, 150, 154–162
  housing, 136, 138, 141, 160–162, 165–172
  long-term care, 147–153
  nursing homes, 136, 148–154, 172–175

Emergency cash reserve, 83, 178, 252
Employment agencies, 259
Environmental concerns, 42–45
Environmental Protection Agency (EPA), 42, 43
Equifax Credit Information Services, 61, 277
Escrow accounts, 79
Estate planning, 125 (*see also* Insurance; Investment)
Exclusions in health care policies, 123
Executors, 129
Expected-contribution rules, 205
Eye care, 144

Factory rebates, 11
Fair Credit Billing Act (FCBA), 272, 273
Fair Credit Reporting Act (FCRA), 276
Fannie Mae (Federal National Mortgage Association), 54, 55, 58
Federal Communications Commission (FCC), 244

Federal Deposit Insurance
Corporation (FDIC), 94,
184
Federal Housing Authority
mortgages, 72
Federal Trade Commission
(FTC), 49, 172, 235, 244,
273, 280
Fidelity, 195
Finance charge, 180–181
Finance companies, 284
Financial aid, 205–206
Financial arrangements
with elderly relatives,
139–142
Financial planners,
193–195
Financing car purchases, 12,
15–17, 73, 223– 224
Fire alarms, 110
Fire insurance, 104
Fixed-rate mortgages, 66–67
Flood insurance, 104
Flu shots, 145
Foreclosure, 82–83
For sale by owner (FSBO),
33–34
Freddie Mae (Federal Home
Loan Mortgage
Corporation), 54, 55, 58,
59
Furs, 107

Gasoline/oil company credit
cards, 266, 281
Gillis, Jack, 4, 23
Gold, 188
Government subsidized
mortgages, 71
Graying of America, 135, 137
Gray market electronics, 227
Group health plans, 119, 120,
123, 124
Guardianship, 140
*Guide to Used Cars*
(Consumer Reports), 15,
23

*Handbook for No-Load
Investors, The* (Jacobs),
199
Headhunters, 258
Health care costs for elderly,
135–136, 142–147
Health care proxy, 142
Health insurance, 114,
117–124, 142–147,
255–256, 262
Health maintenance
organizations (HMOs),
120, 146–147
Hearing aids, 144
Home adaptation, 158–160
Home buying, 25–52
auctions, 49

casing market and
assessing prices, 34–39
condition of home, 40–45
contracts, 39
environmental concerns,
42–45
inspections, 40–41
investment property, 50
mortgages (*see* Mortgages)
old houses, 45
property taxes, 50–51
real estate agents, 31–34,
57
renting versus, 28–30
for sale by owner (FSBO),
33–34
single-family versus multi-
family, 46–47
understanding market
values, 25–28
warranties, 41–42
Home care, 150, 154–162
Home equity loans, 72,
73, 181, 208, 224, 253, 261
Home inspection, 40–41
Home insurance, 102–110
Home loans, 16
Homesharing, 161
Home visitors, 157
Hospice care, 164–165
Hospital-indemnity policies,
118–119, 122

Housing and Urban
Development,
Department of, 44
Housing for elderly, 136, 138,
141, 160–162, 165–172
Hyatt Hotels, 169

Independent Advantage
Financial and Insurance
Services, 93
Independent practice
organizations (IPOs),
120
Individual health plans, 119,
120, 124
Inflation, 29, 30, 50, 114, 207,
208
Inheritance laws, 126
Inside limits, 122
Institute of Certified Financial
Planners, 194
Insurance, 84–125
auto, 11–12, 20, 22, 100,
110–117
disability, 97–102, 119
health, 114, 117–124,
142–147, 255–256, 262
home, 102–110
liability, 108–109, 111–113
life, 85–97, 148–149, 262
long-term care, 136,
150–153, 155, 172

Insurance, *(cont.)*
Medigap, 119, 145–148, 163, 166
private mortgage (PMI), 58, 78–79, 81
renter's, 104, 107
title, 77
Insurance companies, 184
Interest
car loan, 16, 223–224
credit card, 178, 264–266, 269–270
mortgage, 29, 30, 55, 65–76, 179
simple and compound, 183
Intermediate nursing care, 150, 172
Internal Revenue Service (IRS), 246, 248
International Association For Financial Planning, 194
Investment
basics, 188–192
bonds, 187–191, 196
CDs (certificates of deposit), 185–186, 191, 196, 207
college tuition, 176–177, 203–208
financial planners, 193–195
mutual funds, 183, 195–201, 204, 208

real estate, 25–28, 50
retirement, 211–214
scams, 201–203
smart, 196–198
stocks, 178, 185, 186–187, 189–192, 196, 197, 206
IRAs (Individual Retirement Accounts), 212–213

Jacobs, Sheldon, 199
Jewelry, 107
Job-hunting, 257–260
Job security, 249, 250
Joint bank accounts, 141
Joint Commission on the Accreditation of Health Care Organizations, 164
Jumbo mortgages, 58–59
Junk bonds, 187
Junk mail, 236–239

Keogh (H.R. 10) plans, 213–214
Kidney dialysis, 155
*Kiplinger's Personal Finance*, 269

Layaway plans, 230–231
Lead, 44–45
Leaky basement rule, 40
Leasing, 17–19
Lemon laws, 21

Levis, Paul, 128
Liability insurance, 108–109,
111–113
Libel, 109
Life-care communities, 136,
169–170
Life insurance, 85–97,
148–149, 262
Lifeline, 158
Life-support systems, 133
Lifetime learning, 250
Lifewatch, 158
Limited partnerships, 188
Lippert, 199
Liquid investments, 224
Listings, real estate, 31
Living wills, 132–134,
142
Loan to value ratio, 81
Lock-ins, 78
Long-term care insurance,
136, 150–153, 155, 172
Long-term custodial care,
147–153
Loss Leaders, 231, 232
Low-load mutual funds, 199,
204

Magnuson-Moss Act of 1975,
227
Mail-order shopping, 232–235,
237–238

Maintenance, car, 4, 12,
16–17, 23
Major medical policies,
118–119, 122
Marketing Logistics, 195
Marriott Hotels, 169
MasterCard, 221, 265, 275,
281
Meals on wheels, 156
Medicaid, 120, 144–145,
149–150, 153, 163, 172,
173
Medicare, 119–120, 143–145,
148, 154–155, 163, 164,
166, 170, 172, 173
Medigap, 119, 145–148, 163,
166
Military service disability
benefits, 100
Minimum balance, 182
*MONEY College Guide, The*,
206
*Money* magazine, 269
Money market funds, 183,
191, 196
Moody's, 94
Morningstar, 199
Mortgages, 53–83
adjustable-rate, 56, 65,
67–69, 80
bi-weekly, 70
brokers, 61–62

Mortgages, *(cont.)*
  buzz words, 58–59
  closing costs, 28, 29, 59, 65,
    72, 74–80, 179
  commercial banks and
    savings and loans, 59–60
  credit unions, 62
  downpayments, 58, 79
  fixed-rate, 66–67
  foreclosure, 82–83
  government subsidized, 71
  interest, 29, 30, 55, 65–76,
    179
  mortgage companies, 60
  negative amortization, 80
  points, 75–76, 179
  prepayment penalties, 80
  private sources, 63
  qualification rules, 57–58
  refinancing, 56, 80–81, 179
  reverse, 70–71, 136, 148
  second, 72–74
  seller-financed, 63–64
  shopping for, 55–57
  teaser rates, 69
  terms, 66–67
  two-step, 69–70
  VA/FHA, 71–72
Moving expenses, 29
Multipolicy insurance, 115
Municipal bonds, 187, 188

Mutual funds, 183, 195–201,
  204, 208

National Academy of Elder
  Law Attorneys, 142
National Association of Area
  Agencies on Aging, 138,
  158
National Association of
  Claims Assistance
  Professionals (NACAP),
  124
National Association of
  Insurance
  Commissioners (NAIC),
  152–153
National Association of
  Personal Financial
  Advisors (NAPFA), 194,
  195
National Association of
  Private Geriatric Care
  Managers, 158
National Association of
  Securities Dealers
  (NASD), 194
National Automobile Dealers
  Association (NADA), 21
National Charities
  Information Bureau,
  246

National Consumers League (NCL), 138, 166
National Credit Union Share Insurance Fund (NCUSIF), 184
National Foundation for Consumer Credit, 274, 285, 286
National Home Warranty Association, 41
National Hospice Hotline, 165
National Hospice Organization, 165
National Insurance Consumer Organization, 93
National Sanitation Foundation, 45
Negative amortization, 80
Negative equity, 17
Negativism, 251
Networking, 250–252, 257, 258, 260
*New Car Buying Guide* (Consumer Reports), 4
"900" telephone numbers, 195, 243–244, 259, 271, 283
No-fault insurance, 113
No-load mutual funds, 197, 199, 200, 204

North American Securities Administrators Association, 197
NOW (Negotiable Order of Withdrawal) accounts, 182
Nursing homes, 136, 148–154, 172–175

Old age homes, 166–167
Old houses, 45, 104
Open-enrollment rule, 146
Options, new car, 11–12, 14
Out-placement counseling, 256
Oxygen therapy, 155

Paint, lead in, 44
Part-time work, 257
Pensions, 209–211
Permanent (cash value) life insurance, 87–88, 90, 261
Personal articles floater, 108
Personal-care homes, 167–169
Personal liability, 108–109
PERS (Personal Emergency Response System), 158–160
Philanthropic Advisory Service of the Better Business Bureau, 246

Placement services, 258, 259

Points, 75–76, 179

Portfolio diversification, 189

Power of attorney, 140–141

Preexisting conditions, 121, 152

Preferred provider organizations (PPOs), 120

Premium credit cards, 268–269

Prepay college tuition programs, 204

Prepayment penalties, 80, 179

Prescription drugs, 123, 144, 145

Price information on new cars, 4, 7, 9–11, 13

Prime lending rate, 68

Privacy, invasion of, 109

Private mortgage insurance (PMI), 58, 78–79, 81

Probate, 131

Professional associations, 258–259

Property evaluation, 35–36

Property surveys, 76

Property taxes, 50–51

Prospective neighbors, 36

Psychiatric care, 123

Quick & Reilly, 196

Radon, 42–43

Real estate agents, 31–34, 57

Real estate auctions, 49

Real estate contracts, 39

Real estate investments, 25–28, 50

Real estate selling expenses, 29

Recording fees, 77

Reentry life insurance, 90

References, 56–57, 60, 226, 243

Refinancing mortgages, 56, 80–81, 179

Refunds, 230

Renter's insurance, 104, 107

Renting homes, 28–30

Representative payee, 142

Resale value of cars, 4, 12

Respite care, 136, 163–164

Rest homes, 167–169

Resume, 252

Retirement, 177, 208–214

Retirement accounts, 212–214, 261

Return procedures, 233–234

Reverse mortgages, 70–71, 136, 148

Revolving-credit cards (bank cards), 264–265, 281
Riders to insurance policies, 95–96
Rustproofing, 11

Safe deposit boxes, 129–130
Safety devices, 11, 115, 117
Salespeople, 5–8
Savings, 176–178 (*see also* Investment)
Scams, 201–203, 218, 231–232, 247, 260
School system, 35–36
Second mortgages, 72–74
Section 401(k) and 403(b) plans, 213
Secured credit cards, 266–267, 282
Securities and Exchange Commission (SEC), 202
SelectQuote, 93
Seller-financed mortgages, 63–64
Senior apartments, 166–167
Senior centers, 162–163
Series EE bonds, 206–207
Service benefits, 122
Service contracts, 228–229
Shearson, 195

Shopping, 225–235 (*see also* Car buying; Home buying)
coupons, 231
layaway plans, 230–231
mail orders, 232–235, 237–238
scams, 231–232
service contracts, 228–229
warranties, 227–229
Short-term car note, 16–17
Showrooms, 6–7
Silver Pages Directory, 165
Skilled nursing care, 144, 150, 151, 172
Social Security, 98, 99, 142, 143, 177, 209–211
Society for the Right to Die/ Concern for Dying, 134
Society of Real Estate Appraisers, 37
Sound systems, 11
Standard & Poor's, 94
Sticker prices, 10–11
Stocks, 178, 185, 186–187, 189–192, 196, 197, 206
Stolen credit cards, 273
Stop payment, 217, 218
Streamlining, 254
Student loans, 207–208
Super IRAs, 213

Support groups, 136, 138–139,
    259

*Taking the Bite Out of
    Insurance* (National
    Insurance Consumer
    Organization), 93
Taxable equivalent yield
    (TEY), 188
Taxes
    charities, 248
    dependent care credit, 161
    disability insurance, 99
    points, 76
    retirement investing,
        211–214
    unemployment, 255
TeleCheck, 219
Telemarketing, 239–242
Telephone fraud, 242–244
Telephone reassurance, 157
Temporary work, 257
Terminal illness, 142, 164
Termites, 42
Term life insurance, 87–90, 94
Test drives, 5, 23
Theft insurance, 104
Timeshares, 47–49
Title insurance, 77
Title search, 77
Trade-ins, 12, 13, 15, 17

Training opportunities,
    249–250
TRAK Personalized
    Investment Advisory
    Service, 195
Trans Union, 277
Travel and entertainment
    credit cards, 265
Treasury bills and bonds, 68,
    187, 196, 207
Trust agreements, 141
Truth-in-lending laws, 180
TRW, 61, 277
12b-1 fees, 200
Two-step mortgages,
    69–70

Umbrella insurance policies,
    109, 113, 114
Undercoating, 11
Unemployment, 253–260
Uniform Gift to Minors Act
    (UGMA), 206
Uninsurance, 120
U.S. Savings Bonds, 187,
    206–207
Universal life insurance,
    87
*Used Car Book, The* (Gillis),
    23
Used cars, 14–15, 21–24

Vesting rules, 211
Veteran's Administration
    mortgages, 71–72
Veteran's Administration
    payments, 142
Visa, 221, 265, 275, 281
Voice of Help, 158

Warranties
    car, 12, 19–20, 24
    consumer goods, 227–229
    home, 41–42
Water, lead in, 45
Water damage, 104

Weiss Research Inc., 94
Wheelchair access, 159
Whole life insurance, 87, 225
Wills, 125–132, 139, 140
Work-at-home scams,
    260
Workers' compensation, 99
Working Assets, 198

"Your Home, Your Choice"
    (American Association of
    Retired Persons), 162

Zero-coupon bonds, 207

## ABOUT THE AUTHOR

THOMAS N. HEYMANN is the author of *On an Average Day ...*; *On an Average Day in the Soviet Union ...*; *The Unofficial U.S. Census*; *In an Average Lifetime* and *On an Average Day in Japan ...*, all published by Fawcett Books. In addition to his work as an author, Thomas N. Heymann is Director, Home Video at A&E Networks. He holds a Bachelor of Science degree in Radio, Television, and Film from Northwestern University and an MBA in Marketing from Columbia University. He currently resides in Chappaqua, New York with his wife Grace, son Gabriel, daughter Laura, and Labrador retrievers Allie and Grizzly. He has personally experienced—and survived—all of the major negotiations outlined in this book.